THE

SACRED

HAVAMAL

DEDICATION

The Sacred Havamal is dedicated to all wisdom seekers
with courage for the truth. It is for people who can profit
from good advice and don't need the school of hard knocks,
wasted time and their own pain to learn. It is also for the
people who look back on their life and think, "If I had it to
do over again, I would do it better." It is for people who
have learned something in this life. Perhaps this book will
help them pass wisdom to their children so that they can
surpass them. The Sacred Havamal is dedicated to any
child who has had to raise himself and needed the wisdom
and strength of a parent.

ACKNOWLEDGEMENTS

I acknowledge every piece of wisdom that has ever been created, discovered or used on earth. I acknowledge all the people who, by trial and error, great suffering and hard work have acquired and preserved that wisdom for all of us. I acknowledge the original Havamal, which only survives as partial documents pieced together from multiple sources in the 12th century.

☐

PREFACE

It is with great respect and a sense of purpose that I have created The Sacred Havamal. I wanted to make the world's wisdom accessible and relevant by fitting it into life stages from birth to adolescence to maturity to old age. This book can be understood as a person going through life. It sets out basic traits and good habits. As learning moves toward enlightenment, skills can be mastered and character can be developed. Individuals who learn to master themselves can learn to live with reality and progress to mastering relationships with others. The final section of The Sacred Havamal refers to the original Havamal and to ancient runes, elements of knowledge, wisdom and power used by learned people, heads of households and leaders. In the spirit of writing a modern Havamal, I have added over 1,000 stanzas to the original and included all runes of the Elder Futhark.

☐

CONTENTS and INDEX

1
Young and alone on a long road
Once I lost my way
Rich, I felt when I found another
Man rejoices in man
2
The road to wisdom is not easy
To travel it you must first overcome yourself
The highest path, the hardest quest
Growth is almost always painful; alone we seek our goal
3
Live, this is an opportunity so few get; You're lucky
Think of all your possible brothers and sisters
Only you were created, shaped and formed
Made it to birth and now with a chance to live
4
Pain is just part of life, it's nothing to avoid
Life at times can be a pain factory
Pain is temporary, glory is forever, so stay alive
That which does not kill you, makes you stronger
5
Two wooden stakes stood on the plain
On them I hung my clothes
Draped in linen they looked well born
But naked, I was a nobody
6
Little did I know back then
When dealing with other men
That everyone, even the richest
Is naked under his clothes
7
Open your ears to wisdom, your eyes to truth
You have no right to remain pathetic
There is no safety in stupidity
There is no refuge in ignorance
8
You may try to wall yourself off from the world
But you cannot wall off the world from yourself
Making yourself small, hiding and retreating
There is no safe way to avoid life

9
Who am I, what do I want, what should I be
Questions every man must ask; and answer
You are you, here and now, you seek yourself
Answer rightly, what is asked of every man
10
The first step in getting what you want
Is to know what you want
This must be done before anything else
You are you, here and now, what will you do with that
11
This first step takes more brains, work and courage
Than most people are willing to commit
To get what you want, you must know what you want
This must be understood before anything else
12
Forgetting one's purpose
Is the first step in getting lost
Finding one's purpose, discovering yourself
Is the first step in overcoming oneself
13
Knowledge begins with awareness of self
Always know more about you, than others do
The unexamined life is not worth living
Thorough self-examination is a mark of a wise man
14
Be who you want to be
Not what other people want you to be
Only your own desire is legitimate
Only your own goals are bona fide
15
Give me the sovereign man; equal only to himself
The fully emancipated man
Master of his will and embracing of his virtues
Ruler of his passions and commander of his senses
The victorious one who sees clearly and is owner of himself

16
Grant me the sight of something perfect
Something wholly achieved, a man. A full man
A man to justify the existence of men
A man that has the will to become a man
17
What a piece of work is man
How noble in reason, how infinite in faculties
In action, how express and admirable
In apprehension, how like a god
18
I found my path by not walking it and wishing I had
You must awaken, find your path and become yourself
Or you will be dragged along your path
Wishing you had walked it to begin with
19
Too early to many homes I came
Too late to some it seemed
The ale was finished or else not brewed
The unpopular cannot please
20
Some would invite me to visit
But none thought I needed a meal
As though I had eaten a whole joint
Just before with a friend who had two
21
An early meal a man should take
Before he visits friends
Lest when he gets there
He goes hungry, afraid to ask for food
22
Do not forget kindness even for a single meal
Say Please and Thank You
These small words will aid you in your journey
More than talent or beauty
23
Simple things keep a traveler safe
Good habits can save your life
Discipline, manners, and temperance
Are good rules for avoiding harm or vice

24
Smile, look at, and say hello to strangers
Politeness costs nothing and gains everything
It doesn't cost anything to be kind
Good manners befit the son of a king
25
It usually costs more to do ill
Then to do well
A kind word costs nothing
And good manners are free
26
Neither give nor take offense
Do not give offense
Do not take offense
It really is that simple
27
Pay no attention to things that don't concern you
Mind your own business and stay alive
Mind your own business and save your time
Mind your own business and save yourself
28
If a thousand people, do a foolish thing
It is still a foolish thing
Remember, fools outnumber the wise
And the majority is often wrong
29
To many places I fared
Few wise men did I find
Many were fools
Most were not worth a word
30
If you are wise be wise
Keep what gifts the gods gave you
Don't be a fool and don't do stupid things
Many a good man is lost
31
You play the hand you are dealt
Once the game of life has begun
You cannot get a restart
You do not get a fresh hand in Life

32
Each kind attracts its own
Each attracts its own kind
Intelligence seeks its own level
You can judge a man by the company he keeps
33
If you cannot judge the character of a man
If you do not understand his mind
If you do not know what lies in a stranger's heart
Look at his friends
34
The sitters in the hall seldom know
The kin of the newcomer
The best man is marred by faults
And the worst is not without worth
35
To anger a good man; lie to him.
To anger a bad man; tell him the truth
This is a good way to see what lies in the heart of another
You can judge a person by their reaction to the truth
36
At the banquet hall of a stranger
My wisdom was sought, my counsel was praised
In my own lands, none would listen
No man is counted wise in his own home
37
So I left the hall and wandered
But left them no wisdom
Some judged me by my eye patch
Others did not wish to share mead
38
The wise will listen to my counsel, every word
Fare well if you follow it, help you if you heed it
Answer well when asked, it is for you if you need it
And so we may begin
39
Greetings to the host the guest has arrived
In which seat should he sit
Rash is he who at unknown doors
Relies on his own good luck

40
The man who stands at a strange threshold
Should be cautious before he crosses it
Glance this way and that
Who knows what foes may wait in the hall
41
The wayfarer should not walk around unarmed
But have his weapons ready at hand
Who knows when one may need his spear
Or what menace waits on the road
42
A man should not set forth
In the field without his weapons
Who knows what dangers you may find
When one will have need of his spear
43
It is easier to stay out of trouble
Than to get out of trouble
It is better to be careful than sorry
A warning is enough for the wise
44
Be not over wary but wary enough
First of the foaming ale and too much drink
Second of a woman wed to another
And third the tricks and lies of thieves
45
If you are wise, be wise
Keep what goods the gods gave you
Don't ignore five good senses
Seeking an unknown sixth
46
Who travels widely needs his wits about him
The stupid should stay at home
The ignorant man is often laughed at
When he sits at meat with the sage
47
A man should travel
With a companion of equal mind or greater
It is better to travel alone
Than travel with a fool

48
Choose worthy role models
Attach yourself to what is superior
If you find someone smarter than you
Listen and learn from them
49
When to his house a wiser comes
A man of his knowledge should never boast
But rather be sparing of speech and listen
Seldom do the silent make mistakes
50
The ignorant had best be silent
When he moves among other men
No one will know what a nitwit he is
Until he begins to speak
51
Brand kindles brand till they burn out
Flame is quickened by flame
One man from another is known by his deeds
The simpleton by his silence
52
Let a man with his guests be merry
Happy and modest a man should be
But talk sense if he intends to be wise
And expect praise from men
53
Tongue tied is the fool
Unable to open his mouth
The simpleton's speech is tangled
With spirited words, I spoke to my profit
54
Silence becomes the son of a prince
To be silent but brave in battle
It befits a man to be merry and glad
Until the day of his death
55
If you think twice before you speak
You may find that 90 percent of the time
You will have no occasion to speak
Often not even a single word

56
Rather a slip of the foot
Than a slip of the tongue
An open ear and a closed mouth
Is the best-known substitute for wisdom□
57
Silence cannot be misquoted
When you have nothing to say
Say nothing
This is especially true among evil men
58
Omit needless words
Be sparing of speech
If you cannot say something better than silence
Be silent
59
Mother wit is ever a faithful friend
The man is a fool who talks too much
Let thy speech be better than silence
Or be silent
60
Speak in a manner that dignifies you
Your words define who you are
You cannot bring back a single spoken word
No matter how much you wish you could
61
People who would not think
Of talking with their mouths full
Often speak with their heads empty
And to a much greater harm
62
The difference between stupidity and genius
Seems to be; that genius has limits
But the limit of stupidity, I have never seen
No matter how cynical I get, I can't keep up
63
Wise is he not who is never silent
Mouthing meaningless words
A glib tongue that goes on chattering
Sings to its own demise

64
Once a word is spoken
One hundred horses cannot bring it back
Keep your mouth shut when required
A foolish jest may bring about an untimely death□
65
The fool who fancies himself full of wisdom
While he sits by his hearth at home
Quickly finds when questioned by others
That he knows nothing at all
66
The fool thinks that those who laugh at him
Are all his friends and consider him equal
Unaware that when other men talk
How ill they speak of him
67
The fool thinks that those who laugh at him
Are all his friends but when he needs help
Or calls for support at the Thing
Few spokesmen will he find
68
When he meets friends the fool gapes
Is shy and sheepish at first
Then he sips his mead and immediately
All know what an oaf he is
69
Less good than belief would have it
Is mead for the sons of men
A man knows less the more he drinks
And becomes a befuddled fool
70
Drunk I got, dead drunk
When Seer the Wise was with me
Best is the banquet one looks back upon
And remembers all that happened
71
Drink your mead, if you must, but in moderation
Talk sense or be silent
No man is called discourteous
Who goes to bed at an early hour

72

Better gear than good sense
A traveler cannot carry
A heavier burden than too much drink
A traveler cannot carry

73

I have seen ships sink, good men killed
The cost of drink can be high
Greater than a weak man's strength
More than a fool's wisdom

74

Mead is more powerful than some men
Some choose to be its slave
Others choose to be its master
Every man must choose his own

75

A gluttonous man who guzzles away
Brings sorrow upon himself
At the table of the strong he is taunted often
Mocked for his bloated belly

76

The herd knows it's homing time
And leaves the grazing ground
But the gluttonous slob never knows how much
His bloated belly can hold

77

To lengthen your life, lessen your meals
Don't dig your grave with your knife and fork
Too much eating can kill you, as surely as eating too little
Hunger is the first course to a good meal

78

To wisely live you don't need much
Just two simple guidelines as such
It's better to starve than eat whatever
And better alone than with whoever

79

Arise from the table with a small hunger
And you will never have to sit down with one
A man who has learned to master his appetite
Can master anything and will never go hungry

80
To conquer yourself is a greater victory
Than to conquer a hundred in battle
Most men cannot conquer their appetite
Most men cannot control their words
81
A man should be master of his appetite
A man should be master of his words
A man should be master of his habits
And a man should be master of himself□
82
A man who has mastered himself
Is a strong man, his own ally, he is his own sanctuary
He is free and can stand alone
So master yourself, above all
83
If you cannot command yourself
How can you expect to command others
84
The wise man can keep his own counsel
And the strong man is best alone
Solitude is torture; only for those
Who cannot stand their own company
85
Putting up with yourself
Can either be a punishment or a reward
This depends on the quality of you
Which depends on the quality of your deeds
86
He who delights in solitude
Is either a wild beast or a god
87
Every man is the guardian of his own honor
You are responsible for your reputation
You are responsible for your deeds
You are responsible for you

88
Never laugh at the old when they offer counsel
Often their words are wise
From shriveled skin and weary brows
Clear words often come
89
Mock not the traveler met on the road
Nor maliciously laugh at another
Scoff not at guests nor chase them to gates
But relieve the lonely and wretched
90
A man among friends should not mock another
Be not a bringer of ridicule and harsh words
Many believe a good man to be wise
And so he escapes their scorn □
91
The fastest friends may fall out
When they sit at the banquet hall
It is and shall always be a shameful thing
When guest quarrels with guest
92
When you are in the wrong
You cannot also afford to lose your temper
93
Moderate at council a man should be
Not brutal or over bearing
Among the bold the bully will find
Others as bold as he
94
The wise guest has his way of dealing
With those who taunt him at the table
He smiles throughout the meal
Not seeming to hear the twaddle, talked by his foes
95
While I sat at the banquet table
A weak man taunted me
He thought by making me small he would grow
He remained a nobody

96
Silence is the best expression of scorn
97
I have seen the petty fight over small things
I saw a small man distraught over small things
You can tell the size of the man
By the size of what bothers him
98
When Unfreth taunted Beowulf some asked
Why he did not take insult and become angry
But if a person offers you a gift and you refuse
To whom does it belong
99
The tactful guest will take his leave early
Not linger too long
He starts to stink who outstays his welcome
In a hall that is not his own
100
Washed and fed one may fare to the Thing
Though ones clothes be worse for wear
None need be ashamed of shoes or horse
If he earned them by his own hand☐
101
A small hut of one's own is better
A man is his master at home
His heart bleeds in the beggar who must
Ask at each meal for meat
102
A small hut of one's own is better
A man is his master at home
A couple of goats and a corded roof
Are still better than begging
103
It is always better to be alive
The living can keep a cow
The handless can manage a flock
There is nothing the dead can do

104
You become your daily habits
You become what you routinely do
We are our deeds
Adopt good habits, and make them part of yourself
105
You become what is in your heart
You become what is in your mind
Be very careful what you allow to live in you
Shun evil, stay away from the bad
106
An ill-tempered unhappy man
Ridicules all he hears
Making fun of others always refusing
To see the faults in himself
107
Before you complain about your neighbor's faults
Count ten of your own
We often look for faults in others
When we should study ourselves
108
Many men seek to cure
The faults they see in others
Not noticing that they
Are as bad as other men□
109
Clean up your own house first
Before you try to clean the neighborhood
Many fools seek to cure others
When they should heal themselves first
110
Belittle others, to be little
Put others down, to be down
You cannot reduce others
Without reducing yourself
111
Wit should amuse, not abuse
Be gentle and kind with your humor
Be careful with your words
Say nothing you should not

112
Every time before you speak
Ask yourself four simple questions
Is it true, is it kind and is it necessary
And does it improve upon silence
113
If what you enjoy most, is the pain of another
Then all you will have in your life, is pain
You cannot play with the beast within you
Without becoming wholly animal
114
Abusive language is abuse of language
Use language and jokes to amuse not abuse
115
Making someone less will never make you more
And by the same condition making yourself less
Will never make you more
Although it seems, many fools try both
116
Our people perish from lack of knowledge
Lack of wisdom kills our folk
Most people die from stupidity
A great deal of pain is caused by ignorance
117
If the council is good, take it
Sometimes valuable things are free
Some people just know more
Treat a wise man; like a wise man
118
When traveling with people smarter than you
Something is bound to rub off
Associate with people of equal mind or better
If they will have you
119
It takes a wise person to recognize a wise person
A fool cannot recognize his superior
A weak man is uncomfortable with his superior
And an evil man hates his superior

120
A 7 cannot recognize a 9
A 4 cannot comprehend a 7
A dumb person cannot understand or appreciate his better
This is always a problem in lopsided positions of command
121
Better alone than in bad company
Your friends make you and your friends break you
Associating with correct people is correct action
And will lead to a correct life
122
Knots are more easily tied than untied
Be careful what you tie yourself to
Do not take down a fence
Unless you are sure why it was put up
123
Be careful who you allow to be your friend
Be careful who you give yourself to
Be careful who you allow to influence you
Look at who your friends are
124
Do not brag or boast
It is a shame if you cannot fulfill your oath
It is a disgrace if your words are greater than you
Anyone can make an oath, only the true can keep it
125
A true man first does what he says
And only after the deed is done
Says what he did
His actions speak for themselves
126
Fools see the tongue as weak
But it is the most powerful part of you
It sets the direction your body will follow
Life and death are in the words you speak
127
The power of life and death
Are hidden in the tongue
The words a man chooses to speak
Can improve his life or kill him

128
The words you speak give life to deeds
Speak each word knowing it will come true
Don't ask for what you don't want
For you will get what you say
129
Speak of what you do not want
And you cause it to appear
You will achieve what you focus on
You will get what you talk about
130
You will give an account
For every idle word you speak
Choose your words carefully
Every word, every single word, will bear fruit
131
Wish for only what you want
Speak only what you want
Think of only what you want
You will create what you wish, think and speak about
132
Choose your words carefully they have great power
You will get what you give yourself to
Always remember thoughts are things
And words are things
133
Every time you speak
Is an opportunity to improve yourself
Take time to choose the words you live by
Every word you speak defines who you are
134
Be discriminating about what images and ideas
You permit in your mind
Why would you let foul, evil, or harmful things
Live in your head or have a home in your heart
135
Avoid the unlucky and the unwise
They will poison you with their curse
Never share in the shamefully gotten
But allow yourself what is right

136
Be the person you would like to be
Be the person you would become
Be the person you can become
Be the person you should be
137
Learn yourself and master yourself
Your thoughts, impulses and desires
No man is strong enough to fight himself
Every man can beat himself
138
From a short pleasure
May come a long repentance
Consider the cost and long term effects
Of a little or a short term pleasure
139
As a great rock is not disturbed by the wind
Neither is the mind of a wise man
Disturbed by either praise or abuse
He sees both are equal in danger
140
Character is higher than intellect
Character is higher than talent
Character is higher than wealth
Character has the highest value of all
141
If a man offers you a gift and you refuse
He keeps the gift, it is his
If a man offers you an insult and you refuse
He keeps the insult, it is his
142
Always remember, no one can insult you
Without your consent and cooperation
Another person cannot insult you
Unless you help him, by accepting the insult
143
No one can take advantage of you
Unless you allow them to
No one can make you feel inferior
Without your help

144
He who angers you, controls you
145
He who cannot enjoy the gains of his kinsmen
And celebrate the joys of his brothers
Is a foul, greedy, and selfish man
Count him not among your friends
146
Do not impose on others what you do not desire yourself
Treat others as you would like to be treated
Do not do to others what you do not have done to you
If you can do no good, at least do no harm
147
You can't unring a bell; you can't undo an evil deed
Do not do what should not be done
Do not expect others to pain themselves and forgive you
Do not do the unforgivable
148
If you doubt an action is just, don't do it
It really is that simple
Never share in the shamefully gotten
But allow yourself what is right
149
A clear conscience is a coat of armor
The most comfortable garment of all
Men who walk in such a way
Step freer and lighter than most
150
Something done, cannot be undone
Don't be in a hurry to tie
That which cannot be untied
Some actions are permanent
151
Doing someone an evil deed
And then expecting them to forgive you
Is like kicking someone in the face
Then asking them to clean your shoe

152
A man's character is his fate
Your habits are your future
Your present state is from your past
Your future condition will be what you do now
153
What's right isn't always popular
And what's popular isn't always right
A fool can be popular and
Fools outnumber the wise
154
Attach yourself to what is spiritually superior
A man is known by the company he keeps
A man becomes, the company he keeps
A man becomes the thoughts he thinks
155
The job of every young man, is this and only this
Discover who you are, and become that
Do you need to become lost before you can be found
To forget one's purpose is the greatest stupidity of all
156
The secret of joy and success
Is this and only this
Find out what you are
And be what you are
157
If you don't belong to yourself, you will belong to
someone else; and what will they do with you?
Be careful who you belong to
For you will always belong to someone
158
Your dreams are part of you
As much as your arms or legs
Would you voluntary agree to cut off your arm
Then don't surrender your dreams
159
You cannot live without your dreams
They are as much a part of you
As any other part of your body
Do not cut off your dreams

160
A man becomes the things he does
You are your life, your family, and friends
You are what you spend your time doing
You become the life you live
161
Integrate what you believe
Into every area of your life you do not have a right
To isolated, conflicting, or unharmonious, thoughts
Your ideas, beliefs and actions must be whole
162
Conduct yourself in all matters
In accordance with the laws of nature
Going against nature does not change nature
It only perverts you
163
It is better to be what you are
Than to struggle to be what you are not
I learned to be what I am
By not being what I am, and paying the price
164
Live according to your nature
You cannot go against yourself
You cannot conceal your true character
Without paying a huge price
165
You cannot be something you are not
Without being miserable
Without being wrong
Live right and be yourself
166
If you are not doing what you want
You are doing what someone else wants
If you are not doing what you want
You are doing something wrong
167
If you are not having fun
You are doing something wrong

168
I met the chief of the hall
He knew who he was, and
He was what he was
And held the respect of all
169
A tree falls the way it leans
Make sure you are leaning
In the direction, you want to fall
Because sooner or later, everyone falls
170
Listen to the scream of a woman giving birth
Look into the eyes of a dying man
Now tell me that something that begins and ends like that
Is meant for light hearted pleasure or enjoyment
171
Life is too important not to be taken seriously
172
You are more than a seed
Choose to grow and direct your growth
Decide your path and move towards it
Become more than you are
173
Pay what you owe, buy what you want
Then move on with your life, everything has a price
Take what you want, and pay for it
174
The heights of greatness reached and kept
We're not attained by sudden flight
But they while their companions slept
Were toiling upwards through the night
175
You cannot lie or cheat against yourself
You will always lose, you will always pay
You must forgive yourself and face yourself
And everyone must overcome themselves

176
If a true archer misses the mark
He looks for the fault within himself
Don't blame others nor make excuses
Thou shall not alibi
177
No cow ever grew fat from the excuse
Of a lazy man
Don't explain why you are in a sorry state
Beware those who embrace or explain their failure
178
You can have excuses
Or you can have results
But you can't have both
Thou shall not alibi
179
The way to avoid great faults
Is to be aware of little ones
The path of ruin
Is made up of many little things
180
Clearly define the person you want to be
And then become that person
You become what you routinely do
Guard your mind against negative thoughts
181
You are responsible for every word you speak
Your words help define who you are
Your tongue sets in motion
The entire course of your life
182
To live our dreams we first must wake up
And do something to accomplish them
If you want knowledge, you must work for it
Wake up to make your dreams come true
183
The best way to make your dreams come true
Is to wake up and get to work

184
It is amazing how long it takes
To complete something
You are not working on
A moving ant does more than a dozing ox
185
He who makes no mistakes
Probably makes nothing
If you never fail you are not doing enough
If you never fail you are being lazy or a coward
186
The things that hurt, instruct
It seems growth is only possible with pain
At least that's so for fools
Avoiding all challenges will keep you small
187
Even if you are on the right track
You will get run over if you just sit there
You must keep moving forward
You cannot rest on your laurels
188
The fool thinks he can court luck by lacing his left boot first
Luck is when preparation meets opportunity
Work, wisdom, and brains are the only ways to glory
Work hard and prepare, then your chance will come
189
Winning means you are willing to go longer
Work harder and give more than anyone else
If winning was easy everyone would do it
Most know how to win but few will work that hard
190
Polish your blade and make yourself better
After an easy victory do not rest
A wise man will not rely on his enemy's weakness
To make him seem strong
191
Polish the blade after each kill
Gives thanks and don't give into arrogance
The wise man will not become satisfied
But work to improve each time

192
In the simple doing of tasks
There is sacredness
Learn to find the sacred, the joy and fulfillment
In simple everyday choirs
193
What you are thinking about, you are becoming
What you give your energy to, you give your life to
You become what you sacrifice yourself to
So ask yourself, what you are sacrificing
194
He who attends to his greater self
Becomes a greater man
He who attends to his smaller self
Becomes a smaller man
195
Whoever cares to learn will always find a teacher
When the student is ready the teacher will appear
Whatever you are, be your own experience
Forgive yourself, your own self, and become your own pupil
196
Overcome not only yourself but all mankind
What finally comes home to you is your own self
And what you find, what you master, what you learn
Is beyond good and evil
197
A teacher can open the door to which learning can happen
But the student must enter himself
A teacher can only provide an environment
But only the student can enter
198
Example isn't another way to teach
Example isn't a good way to teach
Example isn't the best way to teach
Example is the only way to teach
199
A true genius makes the complex understandable

200
If I give the student one corner of a subject
And he cannot uncover the other three
The lesson is lost
The doer alone learnith
201
Enthusiasm is a learned skill
Good habits are a learned skill
Bad habits are a learned skill
Everything you are, is a learned and practiced skill
202
In order to achieve a goal, a goal must be set
In order to achieve a goal, work must be done
203
You always win when you compete against yourself
Do things to make yourself better
You lose every game you do not play
You are turned down every time you don't ask
204
It is completely fruitless to quarrel with the world
But a quarrel with yourself might be somewhat productive
You have greater ability to improve and change yourself
Than you do to improve or change the world
205
Go ahead and change whatever displeases you
The past is the only part of your life
That you cannot change
Everything else is up to you
206
Ask yourself
If what you are doing today
Is getting you closer
To where you want to be tomorrow
207
Happiness is the result of a thoughtful, disciplined life
Where you are today is because of past events
A good present is the result of a well done past
And a good future is a product of a well done present

208
Be attentive as you build your future
Be attentive as you build your life
Be attentive as you build your children's lives
What you do today will reach far wide and long
209
Remember you become what you practice most
You become what you routinely do
You become the things you do daily
You are your daily habits, we are our deeds
210
The secret of your future
Is hidden in your daily routine
Every outstanding present
Is the result of an outstanding, past
211
Decide to become extraordinary
And do what you need to accomplish that
Become more than you are
It is within your power if you choose
212
Improve yourself in every way you can
You may not be much, but you are all you got
213
Everyday every moment of your life
You should feel that you are getting better
That you have many things left to do
Your greatest songs are still unsung
214
With each day try to do
What seems best for that day
Carry your light with you wherever you go
Our daily deeds make up our life
215
A patch is better than a hole
Even the most unlucky flower
Can at least bloom where it is planted
There is always some good you can do

216
It is better to light a candle
Than to curse the darkness
You can always do something
To help your situation, however small
217
Nature to be commanded
Must be obeyed
When you understand this and obey nature
You can command her
218
The fool tries to drain all the milk from his cow
Thinking only of today, with care, rest, and food
She would have produced milk all season
Some people can't see tomorrow
219
Don't quit before the finish line
On the field of victory lie the bleached white bones
Of those who on the eve of their victory stopped to rest
And there on resting died
220
When something becomes clear, act on it
Once settled on a course of action
Follow through and complete it
Self-trust is the first secret of success
221
A scholar who cherishes comfort
Is not fit to be called a scholar
Too much comfort weakens the body
Too much comfort weakens the mind
222
All difficult things have their origin in what is easy
And great things in what was small
Do today what you can today
For tomorrow will bring its own problems
223
Big things of the world
Can only be achieved
By attending to small details
Little and often fills the purse

224
A big problem is a small problem
That was never handled
If you want to make a small problem into a big one
Keep ignoring it
225
Do the difficult things while they are easy
Do the great things while they are small
A journey of a thousand miles begins with a single step
Avoid the difficult by managing the easy
226
For want of a nail the shoe was lost
For want of a shoe the horse was lost
For want of a horse the rider was lost
For want of a rider the message was lost
For want of a message the battle was lost
For want of a battle the kingdom was lost
And all for the want of a horseshoe nail
227
Do not let your words be empty
Talk in deeds talk in actions
Let your words be actions
Your words should be indistinguishable from you
228
People may doubt what you say
But they will always believe what you do
229
The world owes no man a living
Everything is your responsibility
You could even say everything is your fault
Even if you were simply unable to prevent it
230
The world owes no man a living look how many are dead
Look at all the fine dogs cheated with short life
You are lucky to have gotten this far
You are already living past your fair amount of time

231
Enjoy the struggle
Life is full of struggles
There is nobility in a valiant effort
Don't confuse inconveniences with problems
232
It is okay to feel sorry for yourself
But only for five minutes
If longer you create more problems and sorrow
Than you cure and only make the problem bigger
233
An hour's industry will produce more cheerfulness
Than a month's worth of mourning
234
You might need to create a new life
If you are unsatisfied, dissatisfied with your old one
Develop the skills you need to move forward
Develop the skills you need to live your life
235
To get what you want
You must know what you want
Then set about to get it
To do nothing, is to be nothing
236
Create a worthwhile purpose in life
Create praise worthy purpose to your life
237
One good idea put to use
Is worth more, than a hundred buzzing around
In the back of your head doing nothing
What do you have to show for your thoughts
238
Genius begins great works
Labor alone finishes them
239
Feather by feather the goose is plucked.
Grape by grape the bunch is eaten
Even an elephant can be eaten
One bite at a time

240
The sweetest grapes hang highest
The freshest water is down deep
Sometimes you must work very hard
To get the best, or be the best
240
Snowflakes are some of nature's most fragile things
But look what they can do when they stick together
Fabric is much stronger than its single threads
And a bundle of small sticks is stronger than you can break
241
A coordinated effort is amazing in results
And a coordinated effort is equally amazing in its rarity
It seems most people cannot cooperate on anything
If they could it would threaten the very gods
242
Build in a margin of safety
So that if an accident befalls you
You are still safe
Only a fool relies only on his own good luck
243
A man should know how many logs
And strips of bark from the birch
To stock in autumn that he may have enough
Wood for his winter fires
244
Whatever befalls you, your next move can be good
If you make a bad first move, make the next one good
245
Failure isn't falling down, it's staying down
It's not a shame to get knocked down
It's a shame to stay down
Get on your feet and start again
246
Wisdom takes hard work to acquire
And the process is often difficult and painful
There is no easy road to wisdom
There is no soft way to knowledge

247
Many small opportunities added up
Equal as much as a single great one
248
Every day we are offered
Twice as many opportunities
As misfortunes
A hero never complains for lack of opportunity
249
If you do nothing, then nothing will happen
He who only hopes, is hopeless
250
Joy is an achievement
You must work very hard to achieve it
251
Be good or get good at living your life
You will spend all your time doing it
252
He who would climb the ladder must begin at the bottom
He who would get to the top must continue climbing
And he that would stay at the top
Must constantly work, pay attention and balance
253
You usually know the right thing to do
The hard part is doing it
254
Make something significant of your existence
A life of purpose is the purpose of life
Find your purpose
And you will find your life
255
To know one thing
Is to know a thousand things
If you can completely master one thing
You can master just about anything
256
If you must journey to mountains and fords
Take food and fodder with you
Less you fall and break your leg
And the trip turns into peril

257
If you make your bed and sleep poorly
If you leave your coat and are cold
Do not expect others to save you
From laziness or stupidity of your own
258
You are more likely to act yourself into a feeling
Than to feel yourself into an action
Act the way you wish to feel, act the way you wish to be
And you will become the way you act
259
The purpose of life, is a life of purpose
Unless your life has a definite major purpose
You will drift aimless and directionless through life
 Like a ship with no rudder and end up a failure
260
A workingman earns by his own hand
A wise man lets things work for him
Bees, cattle, nets, ships, work while he rests
He earns money while he sleeps
261
If I cast my net 8 times I may catch 1 fish
If I cast my net 100 times I may catch 6 fish
No one counts how many times you cast your net
Only how many fish you bring home
262
A job started well, is half done
You can have what you want
If you get moving now
Your actions determine your victory
263
Early shall he rise who has designs
On another's land or life
His prey escapes the prone wolf
And the sleeper is seldom victorious
264
Early shall he rise who would gain riches
And set to work at once
The late sleeper loses much
Wealth is half won by the industrious

265
Nothing beats hard work, hard work beats everything
It's the only thing you can control
Others may have greater skill, luck or talent
But it is a shame, if you let someone out work you
266
Perseverance can do many things talent cannot
Nothing beats hard work
267
He who sows barley cannot gather wheat
Think about what you will harvest
When you are planting your crops
Be sure you want to harvest the seeds you plant
268
Take charge of your own destiny
After all it is YOUR destiny
Who else should be in charge of it
Who else should do it, and why would another work for it
269
People who put off little things
Never get big things done
You can never arrive at your final destination
Without taking a first step
270
A little leak will sink a big ship
Pay attention to small important things
Pay attention even to a seeming trifle
A single horse shoe nail can lose a kingdom
271
Always have some project under way
Always be busy doing something good
A busy mind breeds no evil
A person with no good to do, will do something evil
272
When you do not know where you are going
Any road will get you there
A fool can afford to take any road
You must be more careful in choosing your path

273
Energy creates energy, get to work
And you will have more energy
Be tired at the end of every day
From doing a lot of work
274
In every job the beginning
Is the most important part
275
Many drops of water make an ocean
Many grains of sand make the world
Blades of grass determine the prairie
The little things in life determine the big things
276
Good enough, is not good enough
Good is the enemy of great
277
A person's real worth is determined
By what he does, when he has nothing to do
What you do when no one is watching
What you do with your free time
278
Expend your energy for excellence
Don't spend your energy becoming less
Whatever you spend your time on, you get
Whatever you give yourself to, you become
279
If you wish for a thing and do not get it
Try working for it
If you want something you have to make effort to get it
Very few wishes come true, all by themselves
280
A boring life should be feared more than death
The purpose of life, is a life, with purpose
Find your purpose
And you will find your life

281
Every talent that is yours, implies an obligation
You must do something great with great talent
Your ability is the gods gift to you
What you do with it is your gift to them
282
Never give up, never give in, never quit
Keep working till you've won
The first to quit is the first to lose
If you hold on long enough, you will win
283
Hard work beats everything but only in the right direction
The fool who rows his boat the fastest
But in the wrong direction
Gets lost the quickest and goes wrong the most
284
If you want an easy job to seem hard, keep putting it off
Do today what you can do today
For tomorrow will bring its own problems
Accomplish what you can when you can
285
A man who procrastinates
Brings harm onto himself
The first squirrel gets the nut
The second one gets the shell
286
Everyone is as happy as they decide to be
Happy people change what does not make them happy
Sad people find things to make them sad
Then accept their life of pain, and walk a path of misery
287
What the superior man seeks is in himself
And if it is not in him he finds it and puts it in himself
Or works very hard to create it in himself
But usually it's there to begin with
288
If you don't use it you lose it
Your power, your brains, your muscle, your honor
Your love, your dignity, your dreams
Every day you don't exercise something it diminishes

289
Planning your future carefully
Will Save you from regretting your past
290
We become in part what our senses take in
Put yourself in a good environment
Surround yourself with good people
If you put garbage in you will get garbage out
291
It is important to educate the heart with habits to the core
When the mind is exhausted and you can't think or go on
And your instinct and habits take over
You can rely on your heart if your heart is well trained
292
The smallest deed is better
Than the grandest intention
A crawling worm does more
Than sleeping dragon
293
Develop yourself to your fullest potential
To do less is to cheat yourself
With each passing year of your life
Become a wiser, stronger, smarter, better person
294
Always be employed in something useful
Do nothing which is of no use
You can always do a little thing to make yourself better
You can always become smarter
295
No matter how far you have gone down the wrong road
Turn back, it is never too late to start over
And no matter how far you have gone
You still must eventually turn around
296
It is better to have an aim and miss your mark
Than to not have an aim
You will come at least close to your target
Barring dumb luck, you hit only what you aim at

297
Do not slouch it makes you sloppy
Act yourself into a new way of thinking
Act yourself into a new way of being
You will become how you act, be careful
298
Your brain needs exercise to stay fit
Just like your body
Thinking is a task you should do daily
Just like breathing just like breathing
299
Only those who have the patience
To do easy things perfectly
Will acquire the skill to do difficult things well
Have the utmost quality in everything you do
300
It isn't the mountain that wears you out
It's the grain of sand in your shoe
Small unseen weights and annoyances
Can destroy you and keep you from your goals
301
Use your energy positively, if you don't
You must be using your energy negatively
Why would you spend your energy
To hurt yourself
302
Have a purpose for everything you undertake
Do nothing which is of no use
Have nothing which is of no use
Invest your time wisely
303
Most crises present opportunities
If you will allow yourself to see them
No matter how awful the situation is
Look for the opportunity
304
Don't squander your energy
Don't waste time arguing with a fool
Don't spend time in activities that are of no use
Don't spend time doing things of no value

305
Everyone gets the same twenty-four hour in a day
The difference is in how each chooses to use it
An hour is an hour for everyone
Its what people do with that hour that sets them apart
306
A minute lost in the morning
Is not regained all day
Rise early and start the day
Most successful people do this
307
There is only one part of your life that you cannot change
And that is your past, so where do you go from here
Make a good present and in a few years
You will have a good past
308
Doing the best at this moment
Puts you in the best place for your next moment
A well-arranged present is from a well arranged past
A well-arranged future is from a well arranged present
309
Time treats everyone equally
But everyone treats time differently
The secret is, the difference is, the question is
How do you treat time
310
Being happy or being miserable
This is really what separates most people
You must make strategy and work intelligently to be happy
It is your duty to be happy
311
The best throw of the dice is to throw them away
There is no future in gambling
It is a bad habit for losers
You can't get something for nothing
312
After a big adventure
Everything tastes and smells better
The bold experience better food
The bold experience more and better life

313
By pursuing any one of your dreams
You can find fulfillment
Believe that life is worth living
And your belief will create that fact
314
First write your own epitaph
Then live to make it true
You should choose your life
After all it is Your life
315
When death finds you
May you be doing something you love
And while you are doing something you love
May you be living when you die
316
The higher you go the better the view
The view is unique and there is plenty of room
Few make it to the top of the mountain
Why not live here
317
Stretch your mind
Stretch your body
Stretch yourself
In order to stretch your life
318
Don't live life
So that you die disappointed
Live your life so you have nothing to regret
Live life so others will miss you
319
Learn to chase happiness and capture it
Happiness will not chase and capture you
What do you have that happiness wants
Why would it look for you
320
Do not place artificial importance on yourself
Do not congratulate your achievements
Or exaggerate your struggles
By pretending they have cosmic significance

321
The Fates are not humane
They regard all people, all things
As straw puppets, simply to be burned
You are nothing to them
322
Know your place in the universe
You are small, insignificant and biodegradable
323
Never fear death for you were dead a long time
Before you were born, you have already been dead
It's no big deal not painful unpleasant or difficult at all
You've done it before; you will do it again
324
The Norns weave fate not of our choosing
Fate is indifferent to each man's suffering
How you react to fate is the only choice a man has
It's the only thing that sets men apart
325
The decrees of the Norns even when not fair
Must all mortal men bear
But a warrior finds a way to win
Even when the Norns are wrong
326
Action alters fate
The Norns weave each man's fate
But our actions shape our destiny
A hero wins, even if the Fates decree otherwise
327
No great man ever complained for want of opportunity
An opportunity is hidden in every adversity
Every day we are offered
Twice as many solutions, as problems
328
Obstacles are meant to be surmounted
Only the weak and cowards are stopped by them
Walk around obstacles climb or leap over barriers
Crash through walls, there are several ways to win

329
Fences mean nothing to those who can fly
All limitations are yours to disregard
Do not put self-imposed limitations on yourself
All barriers, all limits, are figments of your imagination
330
There is no security, none in all this earth
There is only opportunity
Seize today, put no trust into tomorrow
Plunge boldly into the thick of life
331
You cannot tame life nor should you
It is wild and there is no security in all the world
332
People say grab the bull by the horns
Thinking they are taking charge in life
I say stop thinking small grab him by the horns plus
Get him by the scrotum, if you can
333
Life shrinks or expands in proportion to one's courage
Your courage and attitude control the size of your life
Opportunities multiply as they are seized
The more you do the more you can do
334
What the mind can conceive and believe
The body can achieve
Resolve yourself into being
The master of your destiny
335
Only your mind can make things impossible
All limitations are figments of your imagination
336
What you dream, you can be
What a man can conceive and believe
He can achieve
There is nothing you can't do
337
The very trees of the forest
Get out of the way
Of a man who knows where he is going

338
A man with a vision and a plan on a mission
Is a dangerous man
339
Glory comes to those who mean to win it
And care about nothing else
They take victory as they take breath
And will not be denied
340
They conquer who they believe they can
And think of nothing else
They take victory like they take breath
No man is better than he thinks he is
341
They who win
Win because they think they can
If you cannot see yourself winning
You can't win
342
How can you expect, to win
If you don't expect, To Win
343
A nail can go no farther than its head
And a man can go no farther than his head
344
Your body hears every word, your mind tells it
345
No man is better than he thinks he is
A man can't do more than he believes he can
As a man thinketh in his heart so is he
As a man thinketh in his head so is he
346
No man is better than he thinks he is
No man is better than he wants to be
How can you expect to win
If you don't expect; to win

347
You must go beyond the point
Were luck can affect you
Create your own luck
Make your own fortune
348
A man who can't see himself milking a cow
Will never milk a cow
A man who can't see himself winning a battle
Cannot win a battle
349
Stretch beyond what is comfortable
Otherwise you will stay where you are
Go beyond your limitations, if you don't go past your limits
You will become trapped by your limits, and never escape
350
If you don't get the better of yourself
Someone else will
Take charge of yourself
Learn to control your mind
351
Once a decision is reached, stop worrying
And start on your chosen course of action
352
A man must determine his own course
Or be a thrall
A man must be sovereign
If he is to have kinship with the gods
353
Life begins when you start to understand
Life begins when you wake up and become alive
354
Decide what is worth dying for
Then you will know what is worth living for
And alter your life to live for that
Only the pathetic live for something not worth dying for

355
Assume responsibility for the quality of your thoughts
Your thoughts control if you live in misery or happiness
Assume responsibility for the quality of your own life
You control whether you live in misery or happiness
356
Do not sink to the level of your situation
Respond intelligently, even to unintelligent people
Respond intelligently, even to unintelligent treatment
Respond intelligently, even to an unintelligent world
357
You can't follow two paths
A spring cannot bring forth both salt water and fresh
An apple tree cannot grow corn
You must be without conflict
358
You cannot serve two masters
You cannot do wrong and be right
You cannot do nothing and accomplish something
Your actions, thoughts, and life must be whole
359
Free yourself from hypocrisy
You have no right to isolated unharmonious thoughts
Your actions, beliefs, and ideas
Must be a consistent unified whole
360
Don't ask questions, you don't want answers to
If you ask a question
Be open and prepared to receive an answer
Even the answer you may not want
361
Conduct has the loudest voice
Let your words be actions
We are our deeds
You are what you do
362
Be careful what you pretend to be
For surely you will become that

363
Do not sacrifice your principles to please anyone
You will only displease yourself
And in doing so also displease everyone else
In the end nothing will be gained
364
If you do not run your own life, somebody else will
Who did you choose to run your life
Who are you letting run your life
Who is running your life
365
A person can do more harm to himself
Than anyone else can do to him
It is not the enemies and monsters outside us
We are usually our own worst enemy
366
Face the truth
See the truth, and embrace it
See things as they are
Not as you wish they were
367
Find truth, admit to it
Accept it and embrace it
No matter how ugly or unpleasant
Always seek and embrace the truth
368
If you fear, you cannot live don't Hold on to fears
Fearing death or anything is a waste of time
If you are afraid to leave your home
You're the same as if your too crippled to leave your home
369
The unknown is feared by weak souls
Strong hearts look forward to challenge
The bravest and most courageous people are happy
The fearful and cowards are miserable
370
The babe who cries for his mother
When his share of milk is the worse
So is the warrior who cries
When his spear is the worse

371
The more adventures one goes on in this life
The more stories one has to tell
Do things that add meaning to your life
Build strong memories your children will like to hear
372
Every compromise is surrender
And only serves to invite new demands
You lose a part of yourself at each compromise
The ultimate conclusion to a defensive battle, is surrender
373
Be true to yourself, or lose yourself
The extension of compromise, is surrender
The end result of compromise is surrender
To compromise is to die
374
Don't compromise yourself
You're all you've have
Tough times never last
But tough people do
375
The sun shines after every storm
When you get through your storm
If you are still standing and able to see
Your sun will shine
376
May you be alive when you are alive
And may you be living, when you die
The best way to not die, is to live
Do not die with your dreams unmet
377
To understand life, one must live it
Some fools never live their life
Many are walking corpses
Who are not living their lives
378
Wherever you go
Go with all your heart
If it is not worth putting your heart into
It is not worth going

379
The imminence of death
Should make you live
How much better to live
Long before death threatens you
380
Anxiety breeds anxiety
Worry breeds worry
Fear breeds fear, strength breeds strength
Success breeds success
381
Fearing death accomplished nothing
Live life, fight and love with limitless courage
Laugh at death and when it comes
Know you have lived
382
If you do not fear death
Then you do not fear anything
383
If you are afraid to do something
And do not do it you lose twice
And you are a coward twice
Never make the same mistake twice
384
Fear is the beginning of wisdom
Conquering fear is the beginning of strength
Dismissing fear is the beginning of life
Free yourself from fear
385
There is nothing in the world a man is so afraid of
As getting to know how much more he is capable of
The biggest human temptation is to settle for too little
This is true of almost all men
386
The greatest danger, the greatest risk
Is to not risk danger, is to not risk at all

387
To dare is to lose one's footing momentarily
To not dare, is to lose one's self
You can't steal second base
If you are afraid to take your foot off first
388
Better to make a mistake than to make nothing
For fear of making a mistake
If you are not making mistakes
You are not making much
389
The best teachers trainers and coaches
Smile and tell their pupils to make more mistakes
To risk and try and stretch and learn
And become more than they are today
390
Don't spend your time waiting
If you do then one day you will die
And all of your time will have been spent waiting
Do not wait for anything especially to live
391
Don't wait for the ideal time to begin something
That time will never come. The time to begin is now
If you wait for everything to be right before you start
You will never begin; you will never do anything
392
Seek and ye shall find
Knock and the door will be opened
Ask and you will receive
Most things are yours
393
Confidence outweighs good looks
Nothing is more attractive than confidence
394
The limited are the only ones stopped by limitations
Most prisons are self-made
Envision what you want to be then be it
What we think, is who we are

395
Follow your visions
They should lead you to goals
Which will lead you to actions
Which will lead you to accomplishments
396
Opportunities are made, not found
Find your destiny it will not find you
Every successful person knows
Opportunity does not knock
397
Sometimes you have to go looking
To find good luck
In fact every lucky person knows
You have to search very hard to capture good luck
398
Before wisdom comes diligence
Before strength comes courage
Before honor comes humility
Before glory comes action
399
You create your own future
You create your own luck
You create your own opportunity
You create your own achievements
400
Nothing in life is to be feared, only understood
If you fear knowledge, something is wrong
401
The generous and bold have the best lives
They are seldom beset by cares
But the coward sees danger everywhere
And the miser pines for presents
402
The smith had made a fine sword
But I did not like the price
I really did want the sword
Freya said. Take what you want and pay for it

403
I saw a man with no boat
Who talked of going to sea
He bought a fine house and good horse
But never went to sea
404
You must live your life
It is yours and no one else's
You must do what you want
Or you will do what someone else wants
405
Never rise at night unless you need to love or hunt or spy
Or to ease yourself to the outhouse
Sleep is for strength, rest and growth
Only a fool stays awake worrying at night
406
Foolish is he who frets at night
And lies awake to worry
A weary man when morning comes
He finds all as bad as before
407
Think big, dream big
They are your thoughts
They are your dreams
Why would you do anything small
408
Never react out of fear
Never base a decision on fear
Beware of advice based on someone else's fears
Make every decision and action, on limitless courage
409
What would you do if you did all that you could do
Can you imagine what you would accomplish
If you did all you can
What would you attempt if you could not fail
410
Opportunities multiply as they are seized
Every opportunity grabbed causes two larger ones to grow
Take every small opportunity
And you will never want for a large one

411
Fear is the beginning of wisdom
And when you have gathered enough wisdom
You will have no more fear
Fear just means you have started to think
412
If you don't know life
How can you know death
If you have not lived well
How can you expect to die well
413
Control your habits, or they will control you
Do not give in to your weaker and lesser nature
Be master of your habits
Or your habits will master you
414
Living itself is an art
You should be an artist with your life
You should be your own greatest work
Your life should be your greatest masterpiece
415
Find the things you want to do, and do them
Do the things you want to do
If you are not doing the things you want to do
Then what are you doing
416
Cease the taking of omens
Do away with superstitious doubts
Cease begging to unseen beings
Face reality then until death you need fear nothing
417
Be master of your thoughts
Be master of your mind
Your mind was given to you
You were not given to your mind
418
Observe and feel as many different things as you can
Experience life, before you cross over to death

419
You cannot step into the same river twice
This is because new water is always flowing in
You cannot capture a lost moment
Everything, every moment, is only once
420
Seize the moment
Prudence is a rich ugly old maid, courted by incapacity
Better to murder an infant in its cradle
Than to house unacted desire
421
Those who have not tasted the bitterest of life's bitter
Cannot appreciate the sweetest of life's sweets
422
A bold man is better in all things
The gods look with favor upon the bold
By boldness are great fears concealed
The gods walk with the brave
423
Never react out of fear
Do not base a decision on cowardice
Base all decisions on courage
From your endless inheritance of courage
424
The coward thinks he will live if he hides from danger
Be ashamed to die until you have won some glory
So your kin can raise a stone to you
So your folk can lift a horn to you
425
The timid man can wait too long
The bold will take the things he desires
The first squirrel gets the nut, the second gets the shell
The timid never get what they want
426
Courage is the best gift of all
Courage stands before everything
Courage comprises all virtues
A man with courage has every blessing

427
Valor is contempt of pain and death
Courage champions the cause of right
Courage conquers all things
It even gives strength to the body
428
There is only one freedom and that is fearlessness
Only if you accept all that is life, including death
Only then will you find, there is nothing to fear
Only then, can you do as you will
429
Courage allows fulfillment of the virtues
To not see what is right is stupidity
To see what is right and not do it
Is cowardice
430
More people beat themselves
Than are ever destroyed by enemies
You must first learn to handle and aid yourself
This is the greatest victory
431
Foul thoughts, of loss of fear or tragedy
Or any evil imagining must not be tolerated
Destroy them as you would any dangerous foe
Do not allow them safe refuge in your mind
432
Be, or at least pretend to be brave
No one can tell the difference
Between those who are brave
And those who only act brave
Feigned courage is very difficult to distinguish
From real courage
433
The coward and the hero are both equally afraid
It is only their actions that sets them apart
It is only in their actions that they are different
Act so and soon you will be brave

434
Proceed unafraid
There is no other way
Your heart should be full of courage
Your heart should not know fear
435
Take responsibility for your life
After all, it is your life
Who else should have responsibility for it
Why would you give this responsibility to anyone else
436
Visualize your goals in order to achieve them
If you can't see yourself doing something
You cannot do it
You won't do it
437
Live while you are alive
A boring life should be feared more than death
Life is too short and the world too wonderful
For us to ever be bored
438
If you do not live your life you have lost your life
As surely as if you were killed as an infant
As surely as if you were never born
Why would you throw away the gift of life
439
Every second you are alive
Gives you the opportunity, to live your life
Being bored is an insult to ones self
Being bored is the greatest insult to self
440
Accentuate the positive
You get what you focus on
A person's worth is no greater
Than the worth of their ambitions
441
Courage is the resistance to and mastery of fear
Courage is to live in spite of obstacles
Happiness is a form of courage
It is a duty to be happy

442
Stop getting in the way of your own success
Do not be your own worst enemy
There is no greater enemy than yourself
Rarely will you find the problem outside yourself
443
It is ok if another man defeats you
It is not ok for you to beat yourself
You may beat me
But I will never defeat myself
444
Never let the fear of standing out
Above common men
Get in your way
Of standing out above common men
445
A warrior must keep this before him at all times
At breakfast in the morning, in bed at night
At the spring planting and on the longest night of winter
His only duty in life, is to die
446
Kinsmen be men and let your hearts be strong
And let no warrior in the heat of battle do
What may bring shame to another's eyes
Be strong and quit yourselves as men
447
It is better to live one day as a man
Than one hundred years as a sheep
It is better to die doing right
Than live half a life as a coward
448
One should die proudly who can no longer live proudly
Those who cannot live with any honor
Can at least decide to leave this life with honor
I guess they do the best they can
449
The coward thinks he will live forever
If he but holds back a little in the battle
But in old age he will find no peace
Though spears have spared his limbs

450
Never lift your eyes or pause in battle
Crush your enemy completely
Do not be deceived believing
Your foe is worthy of a chance
451
I will kill my enemy with a club, if I cannot find an axe
I will crush a man with a rock, if I cannot lift a mountain
Quit thinking you can or have go too far
Your opponent can never be too dead
452
Fear kills the coward before he dies
Fear stops the mind and heart
A coward never really lives
His death is not a loss
453
Cattle die, kindred die
Every man is mortal
But I know one thing that never dies
The name of one who has done well
454
Cattle die, kindred die, every man is mortal
But I know one thing that never dies
The glory of a great deed
And the good name of a good man
455
The only things left after you die
Are the good deeds that you have done
The honor you have built
And the good name you have made
456
Acknowledge your fears, write them down
To make them separate from you
Recognize them, visit them, then burn them
And allow them to leave in the smoke
457
Do not accept unacceptable behavior
Tolerance is how far a piece can deviate from perfection
Your tolerance is how far you allow that deviance to go
Tolerance is not a virtue, quite the opposite

458
Don't raise your tolerance to stress
The solution to your condition
Is to fix the problem not tolerate the problem
Living with intolerable things is not a skill
459
Tolerance is how far a part can deviate from true
Before it destroys the whole machine
How far a piece strays from perfection is called tolerance
Tolerance is not a virtue
460
A man cannot live under that same sky
As is fathers murderer as his child's abuser
Some things just cannot be allowed
Justice delayed is justice denied
461
Revenge is the sweetest of all drinks
Sweeter than honey more intoxicating than mead
In all the world it is what the richest crave
In all the world it is what the poorest crave
462
A pacifist too weak to fight is not a pacifist
Someone too weak or unable to avenge wrongs
Is not choosing to forgive, he has no choice
Insects can do nothing when stepped on
463
When one evil comes, a million follow it
If you allow one evil in, you allow a million in
Why would you allow evil in your heart
Why would you allow a single evil
464
It is an interesting paradox we become strong
Only after we acknowledge our weaknesses
If you reveal a weakness it can become a strength
A weakness not admitted is a weakness twice committed
465
Knowing your faults is a strength
Knowing your limitations allows you to exceed them
Admitting a weakness is the first step in curing it
A fault not admitted is twice committed

466
One sign of strength is knowing when to stop
Another sign of strength is being able to stop
Strength become stronger when used properly
Strength simplifies things and makes difficult tasks easy
467
The truth does not blush
A lion doesn't lose sleep
Worrying about the opinion of a sheep
468
The way through a problem is through a problem
The best way out is always through
There is no easier way
Attack your problems and defeat them
469
In getting what you want
You can do things the hard way
Or you can do things, the hard way
There really is only, the hard way
470
Life is not a game, always cheat, always win
Don't play fair, and don't wait your turn
It is always your next move
Why are you playing fair, life is not a game
471
If you find yourself in a fair fight
You have made a big mistake
If you find yourself in a fair fight
You have done something wrong
472
Take advantage, of an advantage
Don't be generous with your foes
473
To win you must first defeat in mind
Impose your will upon your foe
Only then may you conquer
He who can impose his will, will win

474
Wisdom is knowing what to do next
Skill is knowing how to do it
Virtue is doing that action
Strength is ability to complete that action
475
Look back unto your ancestors for strength
They were strong enough to get you here
476
I have been beat bloody and not found wanting
Every time I have come to scratch
True gold does not fear the test of fire
And the truth does not blush
477
You are the master of your fate
You are the captain of your soul
He who overcomes others is strong
He who overcomes himself is stronger
478
It is always darkest before the dawn
Things sometimes get worse before they get better
If you can last through the darkness
You will see the light
479
You can know beyond a doubt
Those heroes you have heard about
Were only men who stuck it out
Until and past their last breath
480
Heroes just go farther than ordinary people
All the heros people sing about
Are simple people who just held out
And kept trying past and through their pain
481
Iron first suffers then becomes a sword
And a diamond is just a chunk of coal
Made good under pressure
The strongest men are forged in the hottest furnace

482
Through great suffering
Have emerged the strongest souls
The most massive characters
Are seated with scars
483
The strongest wood did not come with ease
The stronger the wind the stronger the trees
484
A man of words but not of deeds
Is like a garden full of weeds
He does nothing and is nothing
Empty words are not the weapon to fight with in Valhalla
485
Many false hearts make false boasts
They have no power
If your magic doesn't grow corn
I don't want to hear about it
486
He welcomes the night who has enough provisions
The well prepared, look forward to winter
Unconcerned of swords or spears
Are those whose armor is strong
487
Freedom is a harsh mistress
You must accept all of her or none
Once lost, it will take everything you have
And maybe more than you have; to win her back
488
Do not look forward to the day
When you will stop suffering
Because on that day, you will be dead
489
Children often get hurt
There is no other way to wisdom
No other way for growth or strength
Pain is a harsh teacher

490
The fool who cries for life to be fair
Fights against the truth
The harder he works to straighten life
The more crooked he bends it
491
God is a thought that makes crooked all that is straight
Forcing the image of a fair, kind, loving, caring, gentle god
On to a unfair, unkind, harsh, uncaring world
Forces intelligent men to warp their minds
492
The half-wit does not know
That the world is not fair
One is rich, one is poor
There is no blame in that
493
Profit from your mistakes
Every event either victory or defeat
Should make you smarter
Should make you stronger
494
Remember after you become strong
Everyone will hate you
When you win glory and success
You will win envy, jealousy and loneliness
495
It's one thing to talk of bulls
It's another thing to be in the bullring
496
Only fools and children weep about the past
No warrior ever lost sleep
Wishing the past was different
Even the gods can't change the past
497
When one has not had a good father
One must create one
When one has not had a good childhood
One must relive it

498
Do not dwell in the past
Do not dream for the future
Concentrate your mind to the present
Find the eternal NOW
499
Yesterday will never come again but you have today
When today is yesterday
Will you look back on it with pride, or regret
When today is gone, what will you have to show for it
500
Men who have learned to reach great heights
Are like kites
A kite can rise only against the wind
And the drag of its tail forces the kite to fly
501
Rain and storms make beautiful summer days
And a kite can only rise against the wind
The brook would lose its music and song
If all the rocks were removed
502
Do whatever you will
But first be such that you are able to will
You only do what you are able to will
Be strong enough to will
503
It is the mind that makes the body, everything is mental
In youth I thought the mind was relevant
Then I thought the mind was important
And now I realized the mind is everything
504
You must crawl before you can walk
You must stand, walk, run, struggle and climb
Before you can fly
You cannot just fly into flying
505
Do not be too sad at a loss
Half of your defeat was luck
And do not be too proud at success
Half of your victory was luck

506
Only the mediocre, are always at their best
Luck affects everything, time and timing are everything
The higher highs and lower lows
The greatest have great failures
507
Everyone has demons to overcome
We must always overcome our past
We all have holes to climb out of
We all have chains to break
508
Once the mind is sound
It is easier to make the body fit
Once the body is sound
It is easier to make the mind fit
509
It is easier to behave your way into a new way of thinking
Than to think your way, into a new way of behaving
Use your body to influence your mind
Rule your mind or it will rule you
510
A man who has made a mistake
And doesn't correct it
Is making another mistake
A mistake not admitted, is twice committed
511
Never give into remorse but at once tell yourself
That doing so would only be adding
A second act of stupidity
On to an already committed first
512
Most of the things you worry about, never happen
I have had many terrible problems in my life
Most of which have never come to pass
Don't waste worry on things that probably come true
513
I use memories for my benefit
I do not allow memories to use me for their benefit
Memories are to serve you
You do not serve your memories

514
Control the menu of thoughts and images
That travel through your mind
Your mind was given to you
You were not given to your mind
515
Let memories strengthen you
Use the past as a guide post not a hitching post
Are you a slave to your memories
Memories should be your slaves
516
Change the current of your thoughts if they distress you
Your mind is a gift to you
Use it as you would any tool the most useful tool
Use your brain for your benefit
517
Be master of mind rather than be mastered by your mind
Your thoughts affect your health
Control your thoughts to control your health
Control your mind to control yourself
518
Whoever battles monsters had better be careful
Not to become a monster
If you stare into the abyss long enough
The abyss stares back at you
519
When you have stared into the dragon's eyes long enough
All that is left to do, is to slay the dragon
520
There is no invincible man
There never was a monster who couldn't be killed
And never was a hero who couldn't be beat
Everyone, I mean everyone can be defeated
521
There never was a horse that couldn't be rode
And never a cowboy who couldn't be throwed

522
Whom the gods would destroy
They first call indestructible
Whom the gods would see beaten
They first name invincible
523
Timing is everything
The weaker can defeat the stronger, if his timing is right
Any victory can be won, if you do the right thing
In the right place, at the right time
524
Nothing is given to you in this world
Except the will to take
That which you would have
So you must take, what you would have
525
A fool cried, wishing the past was different
Even the gods can't change the past
Now, is all there is, the past is gone
And tomorrow is not here
526
A ship does not sail on winds that blew yesterday
A once, great warrior now lazy and fat
Cannot live on deeds done long ago
You are only as good as you are, today
527
Fortunate is the man
Who dies at the height of his glory
And never feels the pain
Of one who has outlived his strength
528
The slave must be given food
The free man provides for himself
The world provides for a hero
A god should provide for the world
529
There is no fairness in the affairs of men
The flood may take one house but spar another
The same water that lifts one man's boat
Will drown and kill the luckless man

530
Lance was not the fastest
Nor was he the strongest
But he always found a way to win
Share your boat with lucky people
531
Sven had the strongest dog with a crushing bite
Men looked at his head and jaws to study his secret
His mouth and muscles looked ordinary to everyone
Sven said Rock bites hard, because he wants to bite hard
532
The unbeaten is the untested
Every man can be beaten
Any defeat that leaves you alive
Can be turned into victory
533
Call no man good who has never been tested
Trust ye not an unstained blade
A knight in pretty shining armor
May never have been in a fight
534
The lesser should have no effect on you
When did a dragon ever succumb to the venom of a
serpent
Nor an eagle concern himself with the opinion of a sheep
My breast has never known fear from the inferior
535
The infant cries for his mother's teat
The thrall cries for his luck
The warrior cries for an opportunity
and the king cries for nothing
536
Win as if you are used to it
Lose as if you enjoyed it, for a change
If you win or if you lose, no one should be able to tell
Act the very same way

537
When you are thrown into troubled waters
Choose not to drown but to be washed
Every problem has a solution
Not every trouble should trouble you
538
Dream big
They are your dreams
Why would you choose anything less
Stop making yourself small
539
Heroes became heroes, flaws and all
Don't wait until you are perfect to become a hero
An average man can accomplish outstanding things
In fact all the heros I know except Beowulf had many flaws
540
While in the heat of a fight many men forget to breath
One grew tired he trapped and held air in his lungs
Another always exhaled breathed freely and let his air go
Don't be stingy with your breath, remember to exhale
541
A man locked in a house has blocked all windows
The people outside feel helpless
But think how trapped and helpless the man must feel
Learn to see through your opponent's eyes
542
A fool worries thinking that weak enemies are strong
A wise man can distinguish from
The things that can hurt him to the things that cannot
Learn to perceive and be concerned with only real threats
543
As I prepared for battle with the giants
I realized their size and strength where not my foe
My lack of size and strength are my enemy
Your real enemy is always within you
All battles are with yourself

544
The better can lose to the lesser
The strongest give victory away
Giving opportunity to your enemy
Is more bitter than giving him death
545
Trying to catch up
With someone you should have crushed
Is a bitter battle, no glory
It is a fool's fight and a bitter task
546
You can win only if you're opponent makes a mistake
If you keep your action perfect you cannot be beaten
If your enemy's action is perfect he cannot be beaten
Victory goes to he, who makes the fewest mistakes
547
Plan thoroughly in all your battles, be bold careful and clear
Great leaders are defeated by small things
The first mistake an opponent makes
Is your first opportunity to kill him
The first to err, is often the first to die
548
The mistakes a man gives you
Are the keys to defeat him
The mistakes a man gives you
Is a gift of victory over him.
549
I saw Bjorn's great battle axe
Strike strongly on Armin's shield
It made a great sound but no blood
You must strike so your opponent will die
550
When attacking the enemy
Shoot your arrows between his shields
If he prefers water, use land
If he prefers land fight in the water

551
Do not assume the enemy will not attack
Do not assume the enemy will be kind or generous
Do not presume he will not take advantage
Rely on your ability to win, not his stupidity or kindness
552
Use fire against a wooden house
Use rams against a castle wall
It does no good to strike an enemy
Where it does no damage
553
Two warriors fought in the field
One blocked every blow and grew tired
One dodged and slipped every blow
He carried his opponents head home
554
Man's enemies are not demons
There are many real dangers in the world
And often other people even ones like himself
But most often the individual man is his own worst enemy
555
Some defeats are only installments to victory
When you lose, learn a lesson
556
You cannot keep a good man down
He will constantly seek to regain his feet
It is his nature to rise to the top, like a cork in water
Do not battle such men who never stay down
557
The true are modest in speech
But exceeding in action
A man who has the right to boast doesn't have to
Other men are happy to do it for him
558
Cream always rises to the top
You are as good as your genes
A cork can't help but rise through water
And good breeding will tell

559
Every advantage has a disadvantage
What you do well, can be your undoing
Your greatest strength is your greatest weakness
Your greatest weakness can be used as a strength
560
Learn from your enemy
Learn a lesson every time you lose
Learn a lesson every time you win
Don't learn, only when you lose
561
Success is not permanent
And failure is not fatal
Meet with triumph and disaster
And treat those fickle imposters just the same
562
Make full use of what happens to you
Learn from an enemy learn even from a friend
Learn from every mistake
Learn from every success
563
You are never beaten until you quit
And you are not defeated until you accept it
564
Act with all your might
Do not live your life with half your effort
If you do you will find that you only
Lived half your life
565
You never get the past back
Even the gods can't change the past
No hero ever lost time
Wishing the past was different
566
Remember your past mistakes
Only long enough to profit by them
Never be tied to them and move past them
And always seek profit from them

567
Do not be a slave to your past
Learn from past mistakes and move on
Start over every morning
It's a new chance everyday
568
Remember your ancestors
Use their wisdom and add their strength to yours
Keep your ancestors alive in your heart
Through thoughts and deeds
569
Knowledge is the only difference
In the gods power and yours
A man should increase his knowledge daily
Shameful is an old man no wiser than when young
570
Wisdom is all about learning
How to live a better life
571
Open your eyes and mind
Learn something of every trade
Those lead the fairest life
Who are skilled in all they do
572
The Universe hides things, by putting them near us
See what is in plain sight, see what is important
See what other men don't see
See what other men skip over and miss
573
An experience must be understood
For it to be an experience
Wake up and become aware and alive
Only the intelligent, experience life
574
A life worth living is worth recording
The unexamined life is not worth living
An unrecorded life cannot be examined
And the unexamined life can't be lived well

575
Some people think
The same thought a thousand times
While others think
A thousand different thoughts
576
Everyone is ignorant of some things
But try not to be ignorant of yourself
A man who does not know himself
Does not know anything, and is a poor judge of others
577
The unexamined life is not worth living
A great idea can give your life direction and purpose
The unselfexamined have no ideas, direction or purpose
Knowing others is useful, knowing yourself is better
578
A smart man learns from his own mistakes
A wise man learns from the mistakes of others
Hard knocks and experience are the worst way to learn
You don't have enough time to learn that way
579
Learn from the mistakes of others
You cannot live long enough to make all your own
Fools say time is a great teacher
But remember she kills all her pupils
580
Hunches are usually based on facts
Filed just below the conscious level
Learn to listen to your hunches
Learn to understand your hunches
581
The more you listen to the voice within you
The better it will talk, the wiser it will speak
Hunches are intelligent choices below the surface
Stay humble to better understand what is going on
582
The wise one asked if
I Smelled the flowers blooming
When I said yes he said; you see
Nothing has been hidden

583
A smart man learns from his own mistakes
A wise man learns from the mistakes of others
A fool can only learn from pain
And sometimes not even that
584
The truth frightens many people
Only the bravest and strongest speak the truth
Only children and idiots speak the truth
A remark generally hurts, in proportion to its truth
585
See things for what they really are
Do not be deceived by a lie, trick or deception
Be most aware of what people know as facts
Convictions are more dangerous foes of truth than lies
586
Do not be disturbed at trifles
Small men are troubled by small things
A person is as big as the things that make him angry
A single drop of rain is a flood to an ant
587
You can tell the size of a man
By the size of what troubles him
A small thing should not trouble you
Don't be bothered by little troubles
588
Don't major in minor things
Don't waste your time or your life
On the small and unimportant
Do nothing which is of no use
589
Live in harmony with your beliefs and ideals
Unhappy is the man whose thoughts are not whole
For he must always go against himself
Not being what he truly is
590
You are, largely what you think you are
Even if it is in the deepest recess of your heart
Even if you ignore yourself, and hide it deep
You are still what you think you are

591
Even a blind hog can stumble over an ear of corn
And every dog has his day
Sometimes the stupid, get lucky
On occasion, it is better to be lucky than good
592
Never chose between the lesser of two evils
A choice of two terrible options in not a choice
The lesser of two evils, is the evil of two lessers
When given only two choices, take the third
593
Make decisions based on things you choose
Not alternatives your master gives you
When your enemy gives two choices, pick the third
Know when you are being manipulated
594
Gentleness often disarms the fierce
A kind word can melt the stubborn
A gentle answer turnith away wrath
You catch more flies with honey than with vinegar
595
There is no helping someone up a ladder
Unless he is willing to climb
People have to be willing to help themselves
Before you can do anything for them
596
Don't deceive yourself
Self-deception will end in tragedy
A lie to others may actually benefit you
But lying to yourself will not work
597
Things and people are often not
What we wish them to be
They are only what they are
Learn to accept that
598
There is a difference between
The way things are
And the way you wish them to be
See the difference

599
Real healing occurs in the soul
You must want to be healed, to be healed
Heal yourself, If -you want to be healed
600
What you visualize, you become
Your mind leads the way to everything
601
When I was young I thought the battle was physical
After some fights I thought part of the battle was mental
When I was mature I realized half the battle was mental
Now old I see, all the battle is mental
602
Decisions are easy if you know where you are going
If you don't know where you are going
How can you get there
Know where you are going to make the right choice
603
If little ears should not hear it
Then big mouths should not say it
Often you should not do
What you would not have your children do
604
Do not overuse the word no from pride
Do not overuse the word yes from weakness
Say what you really want
Want what you really say
605
Let go of beliefs that are not true
Let go of limiting beliefs
Let go of beliefs that make you weak
A discarded falsehood is better than a found truth
606
When you get angry
Make sure it is for the right reasons
Make sure it is for something worthy
Your anger should be used, only for a great cause

607
Unite your mind and body
You must become whole
Integrate your mind, body and soul
Integrate your beliefs with your actions and words
608
To know what we know
And to know what we do not know
That is wisdom
609
Changing yourself involves being open to your mistakes
A mistake not admitted is twice committed
A fault confessed is half redressed
A fault not admitted is twice committed
610
There are only two books in life
One of everything you know
One of everything you don't know
Which is bigger
611
Trust your intuition, go with your gut
Your gut sometimes knows more than your brain
If you listen to the little voice inside you
It will become a bigger voice to guide you
612
Never dispute trivial things
Don't focus on the unimportant
Never argue with a fool
Some things are not worth your time
613
An intelligent person listens to everyone
And filters out what is not needed
Never argue with someone you don't respect
Why would you give them your respect and time
614
Develop a strategy for a good life
Just as you would for any successful campaign

615
Sometimes a nap is the best medicine
Napping prepares the mind for fresh thoughts
Sleep can heal, napping is a fine habit
If it is used for production and improvement
616
True relaxation is an art
You must free yourself of everything else
617
Give yourself
The things you need
Small things can make a difference
Give yourself space to breathe
618
Practice breathing
Until you get it right
619
Many people who would not wear iron chains
Will put on silver shackles
Will chase a diamond trap
A golden cage is still a cage
620
Question what others accept
Often the herd is wrong
If a thousand people do a foolish thing
It is still a foolish thing
621
Most of our troubles come from within
You are often your own worst enemy
622
Truth is not beauty
Truth is not ugly
Truth is the way things are
Not the way you wish they were
623
Drink ale by the hearth, over ice glide
Buy a starving mare to fatten at home
Buy a stained sword, choose goods
Which work, not on their appearance or fashion

624
An untested sword, a woman's bed talk
A wronged man, an ambitious man
A weak man, a coward, the advice of a fool
The word of a liar, the word of a foe
Are never safe let no man trust them
625
I saw a family with a sick child they prayed to be healed
They were enslaved by hope, the cruelest master
Hope makes you endure more pain and suffering
Than the most evil human master ever could
626
Only a fool would work his horse while lame
Leave his sword out in the rain to rust
But some men do no better for themselves
In old age their bodies betray them
627
I saw a man who carried a difficult load
He took pleasure in his pain
He ate his poison daily
He did not want to make his life better
628
I met a man on the road
Who did not care for his feet
The next time I met him
He was limping
629
If a dog shits a lot, he won't shit long
If you load a boat too full, it will sink
Carrying too heavy a pack is not a good plan
Some ridiculous schedules cannot be kept up
630
The troll was once a man, who hated trolls
He forgot a law of life
Whatever you concentrate on, you get
He thought of trolls so much, he became one

631
The wife hated her husband so much
She thought of nothing else
She gave him so much of her thoughts and time
She gave him great power over her
632
I sought the greatest treasure, wisdom
As I journeyed many did I find lacking any sense
I wondered how they still lived
Fools and half-wits are everywhere
633
Little a grain of sand little a drop of dew
Little the minds of most men
All men are not equal in wisdom
The half-wise are everywhere
634
Kelly had a dream she did not understand
She told it to a wise friend
Who told her what it meant
Not even the wisest can interpret their own dreams
635
Do not be deceived by words
If it looks like a duck, walks like a duck
And quacks like a duck, it is probably a duck
Even if it claims to be a stork
636
Never hate the truth
If you treat the truth as an enemy
You will always remain in the dark
You will always be misguided
637
Most lies you tell to other people
Start as a lie you tell to yourself
Most people tell a lie they wish was true
And after a while start to believe it
638
Do not believe things that are not true
Do not fall for lies
A lie to others might help you
A lie to yourself can kill you

639
The happiness of your life
Depends on the quality of your thoughts
You are only as good
As the thoughts you allow in your mind
640
Nothing enters into a closed hand
No thoughts enter a closed mind
To receive you must be open
Position yourself to receive good thoughts and things
641
Facts do not cease to exist because they are ignored
The truth does not cease to exist because people refuse it
People's perceptions are not the truth
Reality is the truth
642
Wish to know all the truths
Especially the ones which don't fit
If your belief does not match the truth
Your belief is wrong
643
If there be an omniscient, omnipotent God, then
He is a despicable sociopath utterly unworthy of devotion
644
See reality if your perceptions do not fit reality
Your perceptions are wrong
If your map disagrees with the ground
Your map is wrong
645
The truth is a trap, you cannot have it without being caught
If you actually comprehend and understand the truth
It captures you; you don't capture it
You are changed by the truth, the truth is not changed
646
You can only have the truth
In such a way that it has you
As you increase your knowledge
You will increase your pain

647
Question everything, find the truth, cut out all false
People say more that is false then is true
Make sure you spend more time removing the false
Than you do in seeking the truth
648
It's not what we don't know, that harms us
It's what we know for sure, that just isn't so
False convictions are more dangerous than lies
Losing an illusion is better than finding a truth
649
To be a fool and to recognize you are a fool
Is better than to be a fool and imagine yourself wise.
Real knowledge is to know the extent of one's ignorance
The object of a wise man is truth
650
Do not believe falsehoods
See only what is real
If you can do that
You can do more than most
651
Words are the most powerful drug in the world
Many people can be intoxicated by words
652
To realize that you do not understand is a virtue
Not to realize that you do not understand is a defect
653
By letting go, it all gets done
The world is won by those who let it go
But when you try and try and seek to control everything
The world is beyond winning
654
It is best for man to be middle wise
Not over cunning and clever
No man is able to know his fate
No matter how wise he things he is
So, let him sleep in peace

655
Avoid a man or a god who threatens punishment
For failure to please his will
Trust no god who punishes quickly and severely for slights
Would you keep a human friend who acted that way
656
Beware of a man or god
Who is jealous and wishes to be praised all the time
Only a psychopath is so jealous and vengeful
To threaten torture for failure to praise and please
657
They told me of their god
I struck with my hammer
It crumbled beneath my blow
Be skeptical and test everything
658
There is not enough love and goodness in the world
To waste it on imaginary beings
There is not enough love and goodness in the world
To waste it on an enemy
659
The demand to be loved
Is the greatest of all arrogant presumptions
There is no good man or god
That wants to be praised all the time
660
Always think about things
As they are
Not as they are said to be
Perceive the truth in all situations
661
Every action has an opposite and equal reaction
Every action has lasting consequences
If anything, anything at all were different
Nothing would be the same
662
Sticks and stones can break your bones
But words often do worse than blows
Blows only hurt the body while words can hurt the mind
Words can cause great harm or great good

663
Learn what you do not know
The extent of your knowledge
The extent of your ignorance
Both are equally important
664
The mind must be open in order to learn
A cup must be empty before it can be filled
Just as a full cup can hold no more
You cannot put anything in a mind filled with crap
665
Wisdom is a paradox: it teaches us we have no limitations
But it also teaches us to be aware of the ones we have
666
Choose where you want to live and then look for work
Not the other way around
667
If you put nothing in your head
You will get nothing from it
668
He who knows himself is enlightened
The wisest man is a self-examined man
669
Having knowledge and using knowledge
Are two entirely different things
670
Life is empty and has no meaning
Except that which you give it
So your life can mean anything you choose
What will you do with this power
671
Life has a different meaning to each person
According to what they choose their life to mean
It is wonderful your life can mean anything
What will you do with that
672
Life is empty and has no meaning
Be happy at this opportunity
Great men give great meaning to their lives
Weak men cannot assign a meaning to their lives

673
Thinking is the hardest thing in the world to do
And the most important
And the most underrated
And the most overlooked
And the least appreciated
674
In nature, nothing is done without a purpose
Nature does nothing useless
She is the greatest economist of all
There is a reason for everything
675
People believe what they want to believe
Only looking at facts that support their belief
They even twist the truth to fit their belief
Facts, logic and reason will not persuade them
676
Whatever you cannot understand
You cannot possess
Whatever you cannot understand
You cannot command
677
Listen to what your body says
It is you, talking to you
Be smart enough to listen to yourself
If you are talking to you, listen
678
Your mind can either free or imprison you
Your mind is a tool to serve you
Make sure your mind is working for you
Listen to you, when you talk to you
679
Knowledge also exists when you know
That you do not know something
To know the extent of one's own ignorance
Is the beginning of wisdom

680
Our picture of the world is our way of looking in
Not our way of looking out
Our perception of the world
Is only our picture of our self
681
Whatever catches your eye
For a long enough time
Will catch you
Be careful what you look at
682
Learn from the mistakes of others
You cannot live long enough to make them all yourself
Do you plan to live 10,000 years
Even that would not be long enough
683
All questions will eventually be answered
Even if it takes a very long time
Actually it takes too much time
You will never live that long
684
A problem adequately stated
A problem accurately stated
A problem clearly defined
Is a problem well on its way to being solved
685
One must see a hazard to avoid it
Live with your eyes open
Live with your brain open
Admit ignorance and seek knowledge
686
Sometimes a truth should not be told
Cast not your pearls before swine
Nor give what is good unto dogs
The truth is a treasure many people do not deserve
And they can't appreciate it anyway

687
Sometimes a truth should not be told
Sometimes the people of the world
Aren't ready for certain ideas or are unworthy reality
You might as well give a pigeon gold
688
Be neither a cobbler nor a carver of shafts
If the shoe fits ill or the shaft be crooked
The maker gets curses and kicks
Some tasks receive no thanks
689
The bridge you burn now
May be the one you want to cross later
690
Don't treat strangers as foes
Some may prove their worth
Your greatest allies and best friends
Are people you have not met yet
691
Happy is he who hears words of
Praise, wit, and wise counsel
Evil counsel is often given
By those of evil heart
692
Blessed is he who in his own lifetime
Is awarded praise and wit
For ill counsel is often given
By mortal men to each other
693
Errors start from tiny misunderstandings of the truth
If you know what is true and accept no half truths
If you know what is real and accept no compromise
You will save yourself a lot of trouble
694
Many men labor for things they really don't want
They spend their life time pulling a cart
For a carrot tied at the end of a stick
When they don't even like the taste of carrots

695
Medicines exist against many ills
Listening against feuds, friendship against anger
Sleep against fatigue, wisdom against stupidity
Good food and temperance prevent many ills
696
It is easier to prevent an illness than to cure one
Good honest clean living, is the best medicine
Staying healthy is much easier
Then regaining health and fighting sickness
697
Things and people are often not
What we wish them to be
They are only what they are
Learn to accept that fact
698
If you would not write it and sign it
Do not say it, do not do it
699
The dice cup takes the gold and freedom of many men
Learn to walk away a winner
Learn to walk away a loser
Losing gold is better than losing your freedom
700
The half-wit does not know
That gold makes fools of many men
The riches one may gain today
May disappear tomorrow
701
Trust not an acre sown early
Nor praise a son too soon
Weather rules the acre, and wit the son
Both are exposed to peril
702
Give praise, but not too soon
Praise a son grown, an old bow
An old horse, an old dog
And a wife buried or burned

703
Herds, flocks and fields had Fitjungs sons
Who now carry begging bowls
Wealth may vanish in the wink of an eye
And gold is the falsest of friends
704
The fool who acquires cattle and lands
Or wins a woman's love
His wisdom wanes with his waxing pride
He may lose everything he has gained
705
Ending up with anything valuable
Takes time and careful planning
And remember you are valuable
Make long term investments in yourself
706
The test of a sword is battle
The test of a ship is the sea
The test of a journey is home
And the test of a family is time
707
Create and maintain a peaceful home
He who troubles his own family
He who troubles his own house
Is a fool and will inherit the wind
708
It is right to grieve loss
The death of a parent or child
We grieve the loss that they are not here
Not that they are gone
709
A father tried to protect his children
From all suffering, from all pain
They remained as sheep
Weak, stupid and helpless
710
You can't achieve true happiness
If your goal is to show off
Performing to entertain others
Will not make you happy nor accomplish your goals

711
The good king Beowulf
Knew every action could be used to improve his luck
He sought to go past the point
Where luck could harm him
712
An army of sheep, led by a lion
Will defeat
An army of lions, led by a sheep
713
It is better to be decisive
Even if you are sometimes wrong
714
Cease guessing, conjuring and gossip
Stop prophecy, spells and prayer
Speculating, imagining and assumptions
One look, Is worth a thousand rumors
715
Any fool can make a rule
A society's stupidity and evil is in direct relation
To the number of laws it has and
The number of lawyers and police it has
716
Laws are like spider's webs they catch the weak and poor
But are easily broken by the mighty and rich
Who laugh at them and use them to stay rich
Pretending to help the weak and poor
717
Beware a society in which
The evil and stupid rise to power
Inferior people should never be in positions of superiority
Dumber people should not rule smarter people
718
In a country, well governed
Poverty is something to be ashamed of
In a country, badly governed
Wealth is something to be ashamed of
719
An oppressive government is more destructive to humanity
Than the dangers they claim to protect you from

720
Ruling a great nation
Leading a huge estate
Is like making pie crust
Too much handling will spoil it
721
No nation exists for long that let its women rule
A woman may command but must not govern
They will let in the men of all other nations
And your people will cease to exist
722
A good leader takes the blame when things go bad
And shares the credit when things go well
723
People cut off from their land
People cut off from their kin
Will seek to reconnect with something, anything
And often in perverted ways
724
Feed the soldiers for a thousand days
Use them for one day; War is expensive
Wise nations and individuals know this fact
They cannot afford many wars
725
The superior man is distressed
By the limitations of his ability
The superior man is not distressed by the fact
That other men do not recognize his ability
726
The superior man understands what is right
The inferior man understands what will sell
727
Be careful not to drown yourself
Trying to save a drowning man
728
Avoid the unlucky and the unwise
They will poison you with their curse
No man is strong enough
To fix a weak man, or a broken man

729
If you put a drop of wine in a barrel of sewage
You have a barrel of sewage
If you put a drop of sewage in a barrel of wine
You have a barrel of sewage
730
Don't be ashamed, to outgrow a friend
Do not feel guilty when you outgrow a love
Sometimes it is time, for you to move on
The only option is to remain less
731
Your friend may not want to grow
Your friend might not be able to grow
Your friend may want to remain small
Respect your friends choice and let them go
732
The friend you had while young
May not be the one you need now
You grow apart there is no shame in that
You are a different person now
733
Maybe the tools you played with as a child
Should be put away you have outgrown them
Some people do not grow with you or as high
Sometimes you must move on to become more
734
Do not hinder important business
For the discussion of a trifle
When people talk about the weather
The conversation cannot last longer than five minutes
735
Make the best, wisest and most productive use
Of your time
736
Using the right word makes all the difference
Pick the right words
Carefully choose the words you speak
You will lie or die according to what you say

737
How you say something
Is just as important
As what you say
In fact it's the only thing some people care about
738
A truth that's told with bad intent
Beats all the lies you can invent
739
A good friendship
Makes both people happy
Makes both people better
Otherwise it is a parasitic relationship
740
The loud mouth at the banquet hall
Thinks those who are silent agree with him
And fools who listen also believe this
Sometimes all must be set right
741
Sometimes in the hall
An ill-mannered, rude, arrogant, annoying fool
Is given respect
When he should have been given death
742
Freedom can come from seeing
The ignorance of your critics
And discovering the emptiness of their words
Consider the source and learn to trust yourself
743
Treat a highly intelligent man
Like a highly intelligent man
Treat a wise man, like a wise man
Appreciate what people are
744
He who has endured and suffered much
And knows the ways of the world
He who has traveled widely and seen much
Can tell what spirit governs the hearts of men

745
As you travel you will find
Base people are everywhere
Don't assume the wisdom found in great men
Is common in the common people

746
Not all men are utterly wretched
Some are blessed with children
Some with friends or riches others with worthy works
Even the base may have some worthy quality

747
A man is not what he is
But what others believe him to be
People judge only what their limitations can see
Many a great man never was, never allowed

748
A man is not what he is
But what others believe him to be
Even the greatest man sometimes feels
The small weak boy he used to be

750
No one can succeed when doubted by others
The great are great because, they are believed to be great
No one can do their best work when doubted by others
And no one is good when his watchers are looking for flaws

751
If you put a pickpocket,
In a room full of the most beautiful heroes
In a room of the kindest and wisest of people
All he can see are their pockets

752
A person who has a match
Will find a place to strike it
Beware of giving matches to fools
To a hammer, everything looks like a nail

753
A person who does not know what he is good at
Will not be sure what he is good for
And a person who feels he is good for nothing
Will find something bad to do

754
Every man is out to prove something
It makes no difference who
If not to someone else then
At least to himself
755
Some men after acquiring wisdom are jealous
And do not wish to share what they have learned
They think by giving a little knowledge
Other men will surpass them
756
You could shout the secrets of the universe
From the highest rooftops in all the land
Fools could not understand what you said
Only the wise would hear you
757
Wisdom should be shared
A great work hidden and unseen
Might as well not be
Art and poetry were meant to be shared
758
Do not hide truth or wisdom
Thinking the stupid will become sages
There are no locks on the gates of Asgard
You can't get there, if you don't belong
759
A spoon cannot taste the food it carries
So the fool cannot understand
The wisdom a wise man speaks
Even if he mouths the same words
760
The fool sees the reputation
And a wise man sees the man
Don't see what fools are seeing
See only what is real
761
A wise man is not deceived
By the lies of the outcast or King
Learn to perceive the truth
In all situations

762
Listen to what a man does
Not to what he says
The words of a man might lie
But the deeds of a man are truth
763
Always be honest with yourself
Lie to your enemies not yourself
You may lie to the world and benefit
But a lie to yourself can be fatal
764
Many men have trapped themselves
Not seeing where their actions would lead
By thinking ahead, you can have victory
Don't trap yourself into a corner
765
Men's natures are alike
It is their habits that carry them apart
Keep company only with those who make you better
Those who drag you down are devouring you slowly
766
To some fools there is more joy in anticipation
Than in realization
Some find more joy in pursuit than capture
Some people have no joy in what they have now
767
A disease known and understood is half cured
Part of the cure, is to want to be cured
Some people have grown so comfortable
With their sickness, they want to stay sick
768
Some people take comfort in their illness
Some people have chosen to stay sick
Do not force healing on someone thinking it kind
Ask first. Do you want to be healed?
769
A trifle consoles us because a trifle upset us
If you are upset make sure it is for something worthy
The size of what troubles a person
Is a reflection on the size of that person

770
Almost all advice is worthless
Those who need it, won't take it
And those who will take it
Don't need it
771
It is a tragic twist of the universe that
Those in most need of wisdom, are least able to receive it
Even priceless advice is useless and worthless to a fool
He won't even recognize it and move on unmoved
772
People who can take advice
Are sometimes superior, to those who can give advice
773
A wise man can learn from a fool
But a fool cannot learn from a wise man
774
Telling the truth is a brave act
Tell the truth with one foot out the door
Tell the truth with one foot in the stirrup
Tell the truth only when no one can harm you
775
Be careful not to project
Your values and feeling on to other people
One man's meat is another man's poison
What you value is not what other people value
776
You cannot spoil an already rotten egg
777
The stream returns to its source
A dog returns to its own vomit
Good comes home to good, evil goes back to evil
Everything will eventually revert to what it is
778
A dog does not resent being called a dog
And a pig is beautiful to another pig
Bugs beget bugs, lice breed lice
And kittens grow up to be cats

779
Any jackass can kick down a door
But it takes a carpenter to build one
Destroying things is easier than creating things
Any fool can break a glass or jam a wheel
780
No two people read the same book
No two people see the same sunset
No two men see the same woman
No two mothers see the same child
781
Someone else's misfortunes
Are easier to solve than your own
Many people who cannot fix their own problems
Will tell you how to fix yours
782
The horrible people who are not able to understand wisdom
Tangle up the truth so no one else can enjoy it
Those who cannot appreciate the world
Will attempt to stop others from enjoying it
783
They who cannot bless
Will learn to curse
All cruelty springs from weakness
All cruelty springs from fear, misery or loneliness
784
As there is no red gold
There is no one working to help you
785
Weak people hate the truth
The truth threatens the lies of many people
Many people's lies are their lives
Most people's lies are their lives
786
You cannot win an argument with a child
You cannot win an argument with a fool
Most all arguments are a waste of time
If you would not die over it, don't argue about it

787
Don't argue with a child. Don't argue with a fool
Don't argue with a person whose opinion you don't respect
Don't argue over something that does not matter
Don't argue with someone who is not worth your time
788
It takes two to communicate the truth
One to speak the truth and the other to hear the truth
Both must be wise enough to understand the truth
You cannot communicate the truth to a fool
789
A fool cannot hear and understand the truth
When speaking to people, do not forget this
You may speak the truth, but not communicate the truth
Talking and communicating are two entirely different things
790
What we learn early we remember late
Train the boy to grow the man
As the twig is bent the tree inclines
Give me the boy for 7 years and I will give you the man
791
Medicines were not meant to be lived on
You can become addicted to your sickness
You can become addicted to your pain
Some people have grown to love their misery
792
All things are subject to interpretation
Whichever interpretation prevails
Is a function of power not truth
Always remember winners write history
793
A lie told a million times
Will be thought to be the truth
Even if it is still a lie
Most people just repeat
794
Apologize if you win an argument
Kindness may also win the person
Say "thank you" when complimented, nothing else
Be gracious in victory or defeat

795
No man is so generous that he will be hurt
At accepting a gift in return for a gift
No man is so rich that it really gives him pain
To be repaid
796
The men who take the higher road in life
Will have a lonely trip
The weak and jealous attack them
Sparrows look up and hate eagles
797
The higher an eagle flies
The smaller he looks to those left on the ground
Those who cannot fly
Hate, ridicule and attack those who can and do
798
Becoming more and winning glory
Does not make people love you
You will only earn their jealousy resentment and hatred
No one roots for Goliath
799
A fool thought if he worked hard and achieved great things
He would win the admiration of many people
Success, wealth and power are met with envy not love
Your growth will not lead to popularity
800
If you are strong if you are wise
If you have a good family and are loved
You are a living reprimand, a reminder and example
Of everything your friends are not, they will hate you801
Great indebtedness does not make man or nations grateful
Great indebtedness makes others vengeful
And if a little charity is not immediately forgotten
It grows into a gnawing worm, a poisonous plant
801
A good friendship
Makes both people happy
Makes both people better
Otherwise it is a parasitic relationship

802
Your friends affect your destiny
Choose your friends more carefully than your food
More carefully than your cloths
More carefully than your home
803
Never underestimate the influence of people
You allow into your life
Be careful who you let in
And kick them out as needed
804
He thought himself a good husband
He cut wood and brought home food
He carried his lame wife around, but remember
Someone dependent on you, is someone who hates you
805
From weakness springs every evil and vice
All cruelty springs from weakness
806
There is a foolish corner in the brain
Of even the wisest men
Which will believe the most outlandish things
The wisest of the wise will listen to pretty lies
807
Never ask a barber if you need a haircut
Never ask a car salesman if you need a new car
Recognize when people are selling something
And by the way, everyone is selling something
808
Never mistake motion for action
Many rushing people accomplish nothing
809
There are more worthless people than worthy ones
Fools outnumber the wise
Consider this when dealing with people
Most people are fools
810
There is no such thing as good and evil in nature
Simply different sides, each of which wants to win

811
Do not underestimate your enemy
Just because someone wants to victimize you
Does not mean they are weak or stupid
Smart, strong people want their way too
812
Like a horse that bites its bridle
Or a beaten dog that defends his master
Some slaves defend their masters
Know who your enemies are
813
The best way to know a man
Is to watch him when he is angry
814
The best way to know a man's character
Is to see how he treats people
Who can do nothing good for him in return
How he treats people who have no ability to benefit him
Who can do absolutely nothing for him
815
Only under pressure is a man what he is
Call no man good until he has been tested
Who knows what a man is in his heart
Who knows what a man thinkith in the midnight hours
816
You cannot live on promises
A promise is just a promise
Only after it is done
Does it become real
817
Never listen to what people say
Only listen to what they do
Their words may lie
But their actions are truth
818
You can learn from an opponent
You can learn a great deal from a great opponent

819
Judge a person by his deeds not by his words
His words may lie but his deeds will not
A lie can never become a truth
There is no good deal with a bad man
820
An evil man came to trade I wished for his fine horse
But I did not understand his ways
He talked in a tangled web or words and lies
And it was not worth nine horses to get to know him
821
Liars are usually very good at their trade
Beware when speaking to another
Good liars have lots of practice
There is no good deal with a bad man
822
Bandy no speech with a bad man
Often the better is beaten
In a word fight by the worse
823
If aware that another is wicked, say so
Make no truce or treaty with foes
Do not befriend an evil man
There is no good deal with a bad man
824
Insane positions are not usually replaced by logical ones
But by equally radical, contrary and insane positions
Beware when toppling a dictator or changing a system
Bad often replaces bad
825
Though their clothes be too tattered to keep out the cold
They assure you they can turn lead into gold
Beware the claims of people to accomplish things
They and no one else have ever accomplished before
826
Much truth is spoken in jest
Listen carefully when people joke
If a joke hurts, it might be true
A remark generally hurts in proportion to its truth

827
Stop asking people for things they cannot give you
Never send a wolf to fetch a steak
A pint jar cannot carry a gallon
Know the limits of others and save them from temptation
828
Don't ask more of a person then he is
Don't ask for more than they can do
Many people are less than you would like
Accept and measure people accurately
829
The skillful employer of men will employ
The wise man, the brave man, the covetous man
The stupid man, the lazy man, the strong man
Each has a proper place, even an idiot can be useful
830
The hammer hardens steel and breaks glass
Fire tempers steel and burns paper
You cannot carve rotten wood
You cannot make or shape what isn't there
831
The worst mistake in teaching, is to teach the wrong man
Some men are a waste, rotten wood cannot be carved
Learning does not change the man
Carving doesn't make new wood
832
Carving doesn't make new material
It only reveals what is already inside
Learning doesn't create a new person
If it's not already there, it can't come out
833
Does a mother wrap a baby upside down
After 30 years on the job?
Know what a person has always done
And you know what that person will always do
834
When drunk the truth comes out
Before you sign a treaty
Spend the night drinking with the men
By this you will know them

835
Look for opportunities to make people feel important
Everyone likes to feel important
836
A good salesperson treats you exactly
The way you want to be treated
Treat everyone as if they are wearing a sign
That says I want to feel important
837
He whose words are always fair
Is lying and not to be trusted
838
Selfishness makes people predictable
Use self-interest to predict people
There is not one example of an unselfish act
In all the world it's never been done
839
Use the fact that human nature does not change
To your advantage, this makes people predictable
840
Only the wisest and stupidest of men never change
841
Birds of feather flock together
You can tell a man by the company he keeps
842
A leader is best when people barely know he exists
His work is done his aim fulfilled
And the people will all say we did it ourselves
843
Make your communications so clear that
An honest person could not misunderstand you
And a dishonest person could not misrepresent you
Although you can always trust the dishonest will try
844
Better an enemy than a false friend
Which is why a false friend should be treated more harshly
845
An injured friend is the bitterest of foes
Never betray a friend
But if you must, then kill him

846
Hope is the worst of all evils
It prolongs the time and increases the amount
Of misery a man will endure
847
If you give a person a reason to accomplish something
They will bear almost any how
If people have a reason, to do something
They will find a way
848
Don't bother yourself in how to achieve a goal
Only concern yourself on why to achieve a goal
If you give people a why they will find the how
Passion drives people to accomplish great things
849
Talk can be cheap
Promises made by an evil man
Will not be made true
The words of worthless men are worthless
850
Even the best cause needs a fair hearing
It is good to express the truth at least twice and with a
strong foundation
You must give the truth two good legs on which to stand
Evil men are able to knock down a one-legged truth
851
Do not corner a rat
One of the most dangerous things in the world
Is someone with nothing to lose
Beware of the man, who has nothing to lose
852
A coward will flee if you let him
Don't force him to fight, never corner a rat
If you don't let him run and force him to fight
The Norns might allow him to win
853
The fox flees through the barnyard
The hounds begin to kill chickens
How often has this trick been used on men
Thrown off by the scent of other game

854
A bully at the table
Mocked a weakling sitting there
The weak man pointed out another
The bully taunted the new man
855
Beware the tricks of an enemy
There are so many ways to fool men
But these are the worst and most effectively used
And seem to harm our people the most
856
The greatest trick our enemy ever did
Was to make us think we are our own enemy
Is to make us ashamed, and hate ourselves
Thinking we are evil unworthy of love
857
The greatest weapon against an enemy is another enemy
And the best twist of this trick
Is to make a enemy an enemy of themselves
The enemy who hates and attacks himself how great is that
858
The second greatest trick our enemy ever did
Was to make us think he was our friend
He can also do this while causing us to fight
An enemy he has created for us
859
The third greatest trick our enemy can do
Is to make us think he does not exist
But this trick is weak compared to the first two
The most wonderful weapon against an enemy is an enemy
860
The first rule of war is to know when you're in one
The second rule of war is to know who your enemy is
The third rule of war is to know why you are fighting
The forth rule of war is not to attack yourself
The fifth rule of war, know what you will do, after you win

863
The best act of war is to subdue the enemy without fighting
Get your enemy to fight another enemy
Make your enemy his own enemy
Make your enemy unaware you exist
All war is deception
864
Think outside the box
Or you could lose the whole box
865
The most enslaved people are the ones
Who have the illusion of being free
For even their minds are enslaved
Even their ideas are not free
Even a slave in a cage has a free mind
866
A complete person does not accuse others
Of creating his own misfortunes
Beware those who embrace and explain their failure
A bad workman blames his tools
867
A truth uttered before its time is dangerous
To both the speaker and the hearer
868
Telling the truth is a brave act
Tell the truth with one foot out the door
Tell the truth with one foot in the stirrup
Tell the truth only when no one can harm you
869
Some people demand freedom of speech
When they don't use freedom of thought
870
When cattle are scattered beating the boy who
Left the gate open, will not bring them back
871
Self-preservation is the first law of nature
Realize this with people, organizations or committees
Something told to solve a problem and disappear
Will never commit suicide by solving that problem

872
A man should be loyal through life to friends
And return gift for gift
Laugh when they laugh, cry when they cry
But with lies repay a false friend who lies
873
People treat you the way
You allow them to treat you
And no better than that
No one offers a higher price than you set
874
The girl saw a fine dress and bought it at half price
She would have gladly paid full or even double
She did not realize that the price she set for herself
Was only half of what others would have paid
875
Show up to defend yourself
Or you risk being presumed wrong
When dealing with evil people
Silence actually can be misquoted
875
Nothing reinforces authority and supports authority
Nothing promotes authority and strengthens authority
As much as silence
Silence says everything is as it should be
Silence means everything is accepted everything is right
876
People say they want to help you
But in dealing with people remember
Your mother might love you
But everyone else is selling something
877
Think very carefully
Before you burden a friend with a secret
If you want to keep a secret
Keep it to yourself

878
There is risk to tell a secret to one
Dangerous to tell it to two
To tell it to three is thoughtless folly
Everyone else will know
879
If you tell a secret to one
It must no farther go
Even your worst enemy
Is within six people of you
880
Know what others are plotting
Do not fall to surprise, know who your enemy is
The first rule of war is
To know when you're in one
881
If you deal with another you don't trust
But wish for his good will
Be fair in speech but false in thought
And give him lie for lie
882
Even with one you ill trust
And doubt what he means to do
False words with fair smiles
May get you the gift you desire
883
Odin they said swore an oath on this ring
Who from now on will trust him
Odin explained one morning
Truth and honor will only get you so far
884
Power is at the bottom
Of every talk, dance, kiss, and kill
The honeymoon or battlefield
Are all the same
885
Taunted at the table
I asked the fool to get ale or mead
He though his choice a pleasant one
And left the table

886
It is always your choice
To view a comment as insulting or not
No one can insult you without your help
Consider the source
887
Many men graze their cattle in the glade
None care of your troubles or case the
Fairness of law or the conditions of your cattle
Until his own ox gets gored
888
If a man should come to your house uninvited
For the purpose of helping you
Run from him or kill him
He is only there to cause harm
889
The woman said she loved to help people
People say this is for your good
Many enemies hide in the cloak of helping
While they rob or kill you
890
There is no better camouflage to rob a man
Then to act like you are helping the man
There is no better way to destroy a man
Then to pretend to be his friend
891
People say they want to help you
But remember when dealing with others
Your mother might love you but
Everyone else is selling something
892
He who bears the burden alone knows it's weight
Those who wear silk do not raise the worms
893
We're all in this, Alone
894
Wide is the range of people
Most are in the middle
Gold, poison, iron, salt
You never know what you will find

895
An apple doesn't fall far from its tree
Knowing where something came from
Knowing where something has been
Is half way to understanding it
And can give insights of where it might go
896
I once spent half a night
Teaching a fool his error
It annoyed the fool and made him no wiser
I could have been sleeping
897
Don't try to teach a pig to sing
The pig will never be a good singer
And it annoys the pig
Some things are a waste of your time
898
I watched a man spend half a night
Showing a fool his error
He only made an enemy and
The man was still a fool
899
Most people know their own faults
So it does no good to show them
Most people have lived all their lives with their flaws
So it does no good to point them out
900
The choices are hard if you try to teach a fool
You may waste your time but
If you don't teach a man you may waste the man
It can be difficult to see potential
901
Beware those who use what they hate
Beware those who say they are against
What they embrace
A good salesman loves your money
902
If two take on one they will probably win
Poor chosen words can get you into trouble

903
When out alone remember, two men can beat one
Often words uttered have reaped an ill harvest
Pockets can hide fists, be careful in all situations
Suspect everyone and keep your suspicions to yourself
904
The snake laughed after biting the woman
She had tried to help him and keep him warm
He said you knew I was a snake when you picked me up
You foolish woman what did you expect
905
A wise woman never takes a serpent to her breast
A wise warrior never turns his back to the untrustworthy
Evil should be killed for the good of all
It can never be trusted
906
A leopard cannot change its spots
A scorpion cannot but sting
People are and can only be what they are
No amount of fantasy will change that
907
Be mindful of all your enemies
But living ones are the worst
A dead body avenges no wrongs
And the cut worm forgives the plow
908
In old age Eb was asked if he had any enemies
Left to make peace with or forgive
No I have the finest gift all my enemies are dead
I do not have to settle and forgive
909
Moss is crushed by uncaring feet
But a man is more careful
When walking on sedge grass
Because it cuts back it does not suffer abuse
910
The traveler looked tough so the thieves let him pass
There are easier ways to get gold
Than to getting killed trying to take it from a warrior
Being weak invites attack

911
If you make yourself a doormat
You will be stepped on
Being weak invites attack
912
One is attacked another was left alone
Being willing to fight
Will keep you out of a lot of fights
913
I showed the people how foolish they had been
With spears and swords they chased me
No kind payment did I receive
Tell the truth with one foot in the stirrup
914
Expect people to fight the truth
As they would for their very lives
Many people's lies are their lives
If you threaten people's lies, you threaten their lives
And they will treat you accordingly
You do not win praise with honesty or truth
915
Don't expect the truth to be appreciated
Or any reward for your wisdom
The truth threatens the lies of many people
Most people's lives are built on falsehood
916
I met an old man at the gate
He told me it was easier
For the sun to change its course
Than for most people to change their course
917
It is easier for a ship to fly
Than a fool to admit he was wrong
Or see others are wiser
Or admit he has been a fool
918
It often takes more courage to change one's opinion
Than to stick to it
It is easier to fool a man
Than to get a man to admit he has been fooled

919
If your mother tells you she loves you
Get proof
Nothing is sacred, nothing is sure
Look at the facts for everything
920
As you travel you will never reach
The limits of man's treachery
Nor the limits of his good
See both so you can enjoy and protect yourself
921
It is a rare thing to win both
The argument and the respect of another
You usually win the argument
And resentment of the other
922
It is impossible to defeat an ignorant man
In an argument using logic and reason
You cannot remove an idea with logic
Not put there with logic
923
As the eagle who comes to the ocean shore
Sniffs and hangs her head
Dumbfounded is he who finds at the Thing
No supporters to plead his case
924
Affection is mutual when men can open
All their hearts to each other
He whose words are always fair
Is untrue and not to be trusted
925
Hotter than fire among false hearts
Burns friendship for five days
But suddenly it slackens on day six
Then feeble their friendship was
926
Don't provoke the rage of a kind or quiet man
Some people yell and make a big show of rage
But men who think and plan are dangerous
Beware the fury of a patient man

927
Beware of people who crave power
Beware of people who seek power
They will seek it at your expense
They will sacrifice you to reach their goal
928
I would call the adult crazy and wild
Who would try and reason with a child
Believing little twigs are bent
With calm and reasoned argument
929
Never argue with a fool, never argue with a child
Never argue with a person whose opinion doesn't matter
Never argue with a person whose opinion you don't respect
But most important, don't argue with someone who is right
930
With presents friends should please each other
With a shield or costly coat
Mutual giving makes for mutual friendship
As long as they both shall live
931
The man who does not hold the gains
Of his kinsmen, as though his own
Cannot be trusted nor believed
Count him not among your friends
932
If you find a friend you fully trust
And wish for his good will
Exchange thoughts, exchange gifts
Go often to his house
933
To a false friend the footpath winds
Though his house be on the highway
To a sure friend you make the trip
Though his house be a far way off
934
With a good man it is good to talk
Make him your fast friend
But waste no words on a witless oaf
Nor sit with a senseless ape

935
Two cooks will destroy a kitchen
Two captains will sink a ship
One good leader is worth more
Than a whole committee of geniuses
936
There is no good deal with a bad man
Never open your heart to an evil man
From an evil man, if you make him your friend
You will get evil for good
937
Let sleeping dogs lie
Why wake them up and cause trouble
They are behaving as well as they ever will
938
You can't get wool from a frog
You can't get blood from a turnip
Don't seek from others what is not in them
939
People are such fools
They cry for the liberties they lack
And do not use the liberties they have
I think they just like to do nothing and complain
940
Some people throw off the yoke of slavery
And lose the only value they ever had
941
Women are considered deep because, no man
Can see their depth, no man has seen their limit
This is because they are so shallow
They do not even have a bottom
942
Man himself means nothing to a woman
A man is only a means; she only wants the end
Prestige, security, wealth or, a child
No woman truly loves the man, only what he brings
943
A man is only a means, a child is the end
And any man who thinks otherwise, is a vain fool

944
Fools think marriage and children will make them happy
If you add up all the highs and lows
Children do not make parents happy
You are only as happy as your most miserable child
945
Never seduce another's wife
Never make her your mistress
Strong desire may stupefy heroes
And dull the wits of the wise
946
Never reproach another for his love
It happens often enough
That beauty ensnares with desire the wise
While the foolish remain unmoved
947
Never reproach the plight of another
It happens to many men
Many a man has fallen in love with a woman
In light so dim that he would not have bought a coat in it
948
For this has even happened to me
Deidre called out to me
She bid me come and play
She could talk to me with her eyes
949
So I learned when I sat in the reeds
Hoping to have my desire
Lovely was the flesh of that fair girl
But nothing I hoped for happened
950
On a bed was Billing's daughter
Sun white asleep
No greater delight I longed for then
Than to lie in her lovely arms
951
Come Odin after nightfall
If you wish for a meeting with me
All would be lost if anyone saw us
And learned that we were lovers

952
Afire with longing I left her then
Deceived by her soft words
I thought my wooing had won the maid
That I would have my way
953
After nightfall I hurried back
But the warriors were all awake
Lights burning blazing torches
So false proved the path
954
Towards daybreak back I came
Two guards were sound asleep
I found then that the fair woman
Had tied a bitch to her bed
955
Great shame she made a fool of me
Humility, ridicule and pain
I wished to crawl away and hide
That was all I got from her
956
Many a girl when one gets to know her
Proves to be fickle and false
That treacherous maiden taught me a lesson
That crafty woman covered me with shame
957
The tricks to handle a woman
I never tell to maiden or wife of man
A secret I hide from all
Except the one love who lies in my arms
Or else to my own sister or daughter
958
If you can make a woman laugh
You can do just about anything to her
959
Seem to listen to women even if your minds drifts
Look into her eyes even if you think elsewhere
Even wise women will talk and say nothing
This trait we scorn in men

960
Chase a woman and she runs
Walk away and she will follow
A woman wants what she can't have
Or what another woman wants
961
Follow love and it will flee
Flee love and it will follow
Chase a woman and she will run
Walk away and she will follow
962
Often men seek to win a maid
By deeds that warriors would praise
Women do not value what men value
They only want what other women prize
963
Women count the number of gifts
A man has given, they want constant attention
It is better to often bring many small things
As each gift she accounts the same
964
Avoid a woman who makes you worse
Praise a woman who makes you better
Avoid a woman whose mother you would not wed
For she will grow into her mother
965
She had the shallow, empty eyes of those women
Who ride many man but grow calloused each time
Their intimate ability to love, is diminished each man
Her heart can never be touched or broken again
966
In finding a woman whose charms you seek
But you find her mother is foul
Or you dislike her sisters, or are disgusted by her father
Run away for she can't help but grow into them
967
Avoid the woman who hates men
If she started hating with her father as many women do
She will seek to punish all men
You will be a victim in her war

968
A woman marries a man thinking he will change
And he doesn't
A man marries a woman thinking she won't change
And she does
969
A man wants to marry the perfect girl
Thinking he must find the one
A girl can make do with any man
For she plans to customize and change him
970
This is difficult when finding a woman
The girl you love today
Will grow into an entirely different person
In one year, in ten, or twenty years
This time is unknown, even to herself
971
If you find a girl who acts the opposite of her mother
Simply wait ten years and she will become her mother
She is only pretending to you and herself
Women lie so well they even fool themselves
972
The sweet girl you fall in love with
Can become a hard, mean woman
The deadliest, killing, hunting cat
Was once a playful kitten
973
Kittens grow up to be cats
Cats expect to be served and cats use you
Young girls like kittens outgrow their sweetness
Find yourself a dog
974
Avoid the
weak woman
Who clings like a calf or vine
She is a parasite seeking a host
You can never do enough for her

975
In the hall I was introduced to Karen
A mean, old, ugly, bitch
Strange that the vanity that once came with beauty
Should persist long after the beauty is gone
976
Many women have a very personalized view of the world
And conclude that those things do not exist
Which they would rather not talk about
Fantasy is valued above reality by women
977
One can never know a woman's heart
If she chooses to keep it well hid
Some women are so crafty they fool everyone
They lie so well they even trick themselves
978
It is said that a mule will labor patiently and diligently
Twenty years, for a man he despises
Just for the chance to give him one good kick
And when dealing with women remember
The patience of a mule is nothing
Compared to that of a woman
979
To love a woman whose ways are false
Is like sledding over slippery ice
With unshod horses out of control
Badly trained two-year olds
980
Who knows what governs the heart
That lies in a woman's chest
It is like drifting rudderless on a rough sea
Or catching a reindeer with a crippled hand
981
No man should trust a maiden's words
Not what a woman speaks
Spun on a wheel were woman's hearts
In their breasts was implanted deception

982
An older woman who has been kicked around
Might learn to appreciate a good man
But a younger woman who has suffered none
Finds a good man boring
983
Shun a woman of evil heart
Her bed and her embraces
If she cast her spell you will no longer care
To meet and speak with others
984
An evil woman who entwines your mind
You will desire no food, desire no pleasure
In sorrow fall asleep
She will seek to make you her slave
985
I saw a warrior fatally wounded
By the words of an evil woman
Her cunning tongue caused his death
Though what she alleged was a lie
986
From a ship expect speed
From a shield cover
Keenness from a sword
But a kiss from a girl
987
Never play with the affections of a woman
Tyr has no anger like a jilted lover
Odin has no rage as love turned to hate
Nor Thor a fury as a woman scorned
988
No spear as sharp as love to hate
No storm a fury as a woman scorned
989
Naked I may speak now for I know both
Men are treacherous too
Fairest we speak when foulest we think
Many a good maid, the fairest is deceived

990
Gallantly shall he speak and bring gifts
Who wishes for a woman's love
Praise the features of the fine girl
Who courts well will conquer
991
With a good woman if you wish to enjoy
Her words and her good will
Pledge her fairly and be faithful to it
Enjoy her wisdom and her wit
992
Many men conquer a maid
With more hate then they would conquer a rival
Instead of fists they use lies, trickery and deceit
To put their mark upon a girl
993
Many enjoy chasing a maid
After hard fought victory he wins
She finds his joy was in the battle
In having her he finds no joy
994
Many men after winning the prize
Of a fair maiden they did admire
Find it too difficult to maintain
The false ways they used to wine the maid
995
A boy gives love to get sex
A girl gives sex to get love
A woman needs a reason
A man only needs a place
996
A boy will talk to a girl to get sex
A girl will give sex to be talked to
Many a young maid is so desperate for attention
She will do anything and trade anything to get it
997
Man should be a warrior, lover, poet and king
Provider protector adventurer comforter and strong
Some men are not strong enough to be a man
Often women give up on finding a man

998
Date for fun, marry for life
The funniest dates are not the finest mates
999
If entering marriage ask
Will I enjoy conversation with this person in old age
This is where all marriages end
Everything else in marriage is transitory
1000
A marriage bound by beauty
Lasts only as long as the beauty
1001
Don't get involved with a person
Who has more problems than you
1002
True love cannot exist, without friendship first
If you don't like someone well enough to be their friend
Why would you think you could love them
What makes you think you could build a life with them
1003
A lover's faults cannot bother you
If they do, then find another lover
No one is without faults
In marriage, a person has to live with twice as many faults
1004
Pretending to be in love will make you less happy
Than not being in love
Love occurs less often
Than most people will admit
1005
Fear of being alone creates more marriages than love
Many a heart is caught on the rebound
Fear and loneliness cause
More marriages than love
1006
It is better to love someone you cannot have
Than to have someone you cannot love
Pretending to be in love
Will cause you more pain than not having love

1007
Hate is not the opposite of love
The thinnest line is between love and hate
Apathy is the opposite of love
Love and hate are two sides of the same coin
1008
It takes two people to make a marriage work
But it only takes one to make it fail
Marriage is like a big log carried by two people
If either lets go of their end it falls to the ground
One person cannot keep both sides up in the air
It takes two people to hold a rope tight
But if either drop their end the rope like a marriage falls
1009
A good marriage is made up of two good people
Who both love each other
Who both want the same things out of life
Who each holds up their end of the marriage
1010
a marriage can work only if both work
If either let's go of their end the marriage fails
It takes two to make a marriage work
But it only takes one to make it fail
1011
Life is pleasant if you choose the right companion
A good marriage first starts with two good people
Finding two good people is rare enough
But those two people with the same goals working together
Very rare indeed
1012
A happy journey almost always depends
On choosing the right partner
A happy marriage almost always depends
On choosing the right partner
1013
Of all the decisions of life this is one of the most important
There is no hope for a man who can't marry up
The greatest goal of the greatest man, is to marry up
I can't respect a man who can't marry up

1014
After love is accepted, it becomes
Twice as strong as love only given
1015
In marriage, the problem is not how well you get along
It's how well you don't get along
If the good times are good. So what?
Only with the right person can disagreements end well
1016
Absence is like the wind for lovers apart
It can put out a small weak fire
But fans a great flame to burn even hotter
If distance destroys your love, it wasn't love
1017
Two people loving equally
Is a rare occurrence
To have a good marriage
You must have two good people
1018
It is all right to love someone
More than they love you
Simple math will tell you
Half the people in the world do
1019
When love stops growing, it dies
When passion fades, replace it with compassion
It is not lack of love that makes marriages fail
But lack of friendship
1020
A good mate is more hard to find than treasure
And worth more
Selection of a wrong mate
Has ruined many lives
1021
A good marriage is like most fine things
It gets better with time

1022
A marriage between two people is like carrying a heavy log
If either drops his end, it falls
It takes two people to make a marriage work
But only one to make it fail
1023
Treasure your spouse
Treasure your mate and marriage
They are the most valuable things you have
They should be the most important thing to you
1024
Do not keep love a secret
The person you love ought to know it
Otherwise it is a waste
Important things must be said
1025
Don't conceal love, in all the world
It is one of the most beautiful things
To hide it is a shame
The wisest people know how to love
1026
Everyone in love is beautiful
When you love someone you get to live two lives
1027
Wife and mother is the ultimate career
All other careers exist simply to support it
1028
Moderation in all things
Even moderation
Moderation in all things
Except love
1029
A thousand candles can be lit from one candle
Love happiness and joy do not diminish by sharing them
1030
How can anyone else like you, if you do not like you
How can anyone love you, if you do not love you

1031
The reward of love, is love
Love is its own reward
If you do not understand this
There is nothing I can say to you
1032
A walk helps the inside as well as the outside
A walk can be a moving meditation
There are no problems
That you cannot walk away from
1033
Many great truths, many great thoughts
Are conceived, by walking
1034
Allow a walk to empty your mind
Allow a walk to cleanse your mind
Allow a walk to fill your mind
A walk is good for so many things
1035
He who knows enough is enough
Will always have enough
1036
Be happy while you are alive
For you are a long-time dead
1037
Content yourself
With being a lover of wisdom
And a seeker of truth
Life is easy when it is simple
1038
Life can become so complicated and busy
That sometimes you forget to live
1039
A balanced life needs to combine
The past, the present, and the future
1040
Much anxiety is caused by worry over the future
Much depression is caused by worry over the past
How much sadness is caused by something
That is gone or may never come

1041
Greed, envy and jealousy
To satisfy these emotions might feel good
How good it feels to scratch an itch
How much better it is to never have an itch
1042
Fill your life with love
Fill your life with joy
Fill your life with good things
That way there is no room for bad
1043
Every day, it is your duty
To make the rest of your life
The best of your life
There is no other way to live
1044
Spend more energy on the things that make you happy
Spend less energy on the things that make you unhappy
Life really is that simple
But you insist on making it complicated
1045
When you are hungry eat, when you are tired sleep
Drink when you are thirsty
Fools will laugh at me
But wise men know what I mean
1046
The simple joys in life are precious
The sight of the sun after a storm
The smell of flowers after a rain
The taste of water when you are thirsty
1047
These things are thought best
Fire when cold, a child's laugh
Good health and the gifts to keep it
And a life that avoids vice
1048
It is a gift to lead a simple life, find joy in everyday things
Simple clean living, is the foundation for the best lives

1049
Discover the essential things
And see if they are missing from your life
Then you can put them in your life
Then you can make your life whole
1050
He who binds to himself a joy
Doth the winged thing destroy
He who kisses joy as it flies
Lives in eternity's sunrise
1051
It's better to embrace a moment and enjoy it
Than to destroy a moment by trying to trap and keep it
Worry or fear of losing the moment
Will destroy the moment
1052
Some of the most wonderful things in life
Were not meant to last forever
1053
The moving finger writes and having writ moves on
Not all your piety, nor wit
Shall lure it back, to cancel half a line
Nor all your tears, wash out, a word of it
1054
A great dessert can wipe away
The taste of a bad meal
1055
You can ruin the present
By worrying about the future
You can ruin the present
By worrying about the past
He who has now, has everything
1056
Be content with what you have
Rejoice in the way things are
When you realize there is nothing lacking
The whole world belongs to you

1057
Memories are your most valuable possessions
You should spend a lifetime building that treasure
Spend your time, making good memories
Remembering happiness is like enjoying it twice
1058
Thoughts can make you more ill, than any germ
Good thoughts are half of health
Good thoughts are half of wealth
Good thoughts are half of happiness
Learn to control your thoughts
1059
We travel the world to find the beautiful
But at the end of the journey find
We must carry beauty within ourselves
Happiness can only be found within
1060
Life is not a goal to accomplish or a job to finish
It is a journey that you must enjoy along the way
Wake up and appreciate everything you encounter
Be good, live and be happy today
1061
Remember the value of time
Time is the most valuable thing you have
Time is the most expensive thing you have or can spend
Time is the your most precious commodity
1062
Read the best books first
Eat dessert first, eat off of your finest china
Eat the sweetest apples out of the barrel first
And you will always eat the best
Do not wait to experience good things

1063
After the fall harvest I got a large beautiful barrel of apples
I saw one with a bad spot so ate it quickly and first
Then another and another, and another
I continued to rid myself of the blemished ones this way
In the spring at the end of that delicious barrel
I realized I had done nothing
But eat rotten apples all winter
If only I had thrown that first bad one away
1064
The only thing we truly possess in life is time
Make sure your time is valuable
By filling your time with very good things
1065
Time is said to go by, but you go by, not time
Time waits for no man
1066
The greatest gift to give someone
Is the gift of your time
Be sure you are worthy to present it
Be sure they are worthy if you offer it
1067
Anyone who dares to waste one hour of life
Has not yet learned the value of life
1068
Nothing is worth more than this day
Life begins every morning
Soak each day up like a sponge
The time to be happy, is now
1069
Have passion for at least one thing
And have interest in a thousand things
1070
Take time to live
Don't wait for the verge of death
Before you begin to live

1071
Every minute counts
Every second counts
Do not waste a single moment
Of your precious life
1072
He who has now, has eternity
He who lives in the present, lives in eternity
Learn to live in the present moment
Every day is a lifetime
1073
I have had many great problems in my life
Most of which have never come to pass
Worrying about what might happen or might not happen
Wastes a lot of time, wastes a lot of life
1074
The greatest use of life
Is to spend it on something
That will outlast you
Invest in something, greater than you
1075
Share your gifts with others
And it will be returned to you one hundred times
A hand that gives also gathers
A closed hand gathers nothing and a fist cannot receive
1076
He who hoards has little
He who gives has much
He who is full of himself
Is empty
1077
Anger punishes itself
Envy eats up the jealous
The covetous man is his own tormentor
To stay angry, is to punish yourself
1078
Money often costs too much
It may cost too much and take too much time
To earn money
Keep in perspective the value of money

1079
A rising tide lifts all boats
A bountiful harvest helps everyone
1080
A good bargain is no bargain
If you do not need the thing
It is too hard to work for money
To spend it on things you really don't need
1081
He who buys what he does not need
Steals from himself
If you buy what you do not need
No matter how cheap it will cost you dearly
1082
Many troubles are avoided by leading a simple life
Every possession you have implies a responsibility
Everything you own, also owns you
Everything you have, also has you
1083
Halving your wants doubles your wealth
You can double your possessions by halving your wants
Having what you want, and wanting what you have
Are the same thing
1084
Too few know when they possess enough
Fewer still know how to enjoy it
1085
Charm can be used as a key
Which can open almost any lock
1086
Get rid of all the extras
If something is of no use
Do not burden yourself with it
Get rid of it, let go
1087
Get what you want, then enjoy it
Take what you want, and pay for it

1088
You may have to forgo wealth and power
If you want to attain happiness and freedom
You may have to forgo revenge
If you want to attain wealth and happiness
1089
By having fewer wants you come closer to knowing yourself
Decide what is important in life and disregard the rest
Teach yourself to have fewer wants
Teach yourself to enjoy what you have
1090
The man is richest whose pleasures are simplest
The greatest of all riches, is not desiring them
1091
The mind alone know what is near the heart
Each is his own judge
The worst sickness for a wise man
Is to crave what he cannot enjoy
1091
Envy can consume the envious
To want what another has
Is a poisonous painful noxious weed
Which never seems to stop growing□
1092
The wisdom of life can consist
In the elimination of nonessentials
1093
Anything nonessential in your life, is taking
The place of something essential in your life
1094
New things become used things
The very next day
1095
For everything you have missed
You have gained something else
For everything you gain
You lose something

1096
The wise do not want
The things the unwise crave
Be superior to your possessions
Be more powerful than your cravings
1097
To know when you have enough
Is to be rich
Few know when they possess enough
And fewer still know how to enjoy what they have
1098
Every possession implies a duty
Every right implies a responsibility
1099
Neither abstinence nor excess renders a man happy
Too little or too much, spoils everything
1100
Joy is the ability to be happy in small things
Make happiness a habit, make yourself happy everyday
Hold yourself responsible for the way you feel
You are accountable for the way you feel
1101
Life becomes less complex
When you eliminate needless wants
Do not fill your house
With what you do not want, use or need
1102
Have nothing in your home
Which you do not know to be useful or beautiful
1103
The more possessions you have
The more worries you have
Everything you possess
Also possesses you
1104
Before buying anything
Ask if you can do without it
Free yourself from the things
You don't want or need

1105
Much happiness is overlooked
Because it does not cost anything
Few things worth having can be purchased
1106
Emotional needs can never be satisfied
By material items
The most important things in life
Cannot be bought
1107
Work should not be done for money alone
Not everything that can be counted, counts
And not everything that counts, can be counted
Some of the best things in life are not measured in money
1108
The more material things you have
The less freedom you have
Don't let your possessions
Possess you
1109
Once he has won wealth enough
A man should not crave for more
What he saves for friends, foes may take
Hopes are often not manifested
1110
Go through life feeling neither greed nor envy
1111
Envy accomplishes nothing
Greed gains nothing
Strife protects nothing
Jealously keeps nothing
1112
The more content you are with yourself
The less you want and the more you have
Your wants should be easily supplied
1113
Nothing can make a person happy
But that which comes from within
Don't expect things outside yourself to make you happy
You are about as happy, as you decide to be

1114
Every moment of your life
You should feel that you are getting better
That you have many things left to do
Your greatest songs are still unsung
1115
Health is the greatest possession
Contentment is the greatest treasure
Confidence is the greatest friend
Non-attachment is the greatest joy
1116
Health is the greatest of human blessings
Good health requires that you
Have your body, mind, and soul in balance
Good thoughts are half of health
1117
Life is far too short
And the world far too grand
For us to ever be bored
For us to ever have nothing to do
1118
Celebrate being alive, every act you commit
Should be a celebration of your life
Each day set aside some time for fun
Joy happiness and fun should be a priority
1119
Exercise your soul
Exercise your mind
Exercise your body
Do not neglect anything
1120
Use technology to simplify your life and make it better
Not complicate your life and make it worse
1121
Smiling and laughing are cheaper
Than make up, dye or plastic surgery
If you are too busy to smile and laugh
You are too busy

1122
Get rid of everything that isn't good for you
If something or someone is not helping you
It is hurting you, in the very least it is in place of
Something that could be helping you
1123
It does not profit a man to gain the entire world
But lose himself
Working for false things outside yourself
Usually doesn't help things inside yourself
1124
Enforce family rules, children suffer from no boundaries
Too many choices pains a child
Give your children the security of limits
Children feel safer with strong boundaries
1125
Surround yourself with
People, colors, sounds, things and work
That nourish you
To do otherwise is to starve your soul
1126
Friendship with yourself is needed
Before you can be a friend to anyone else
Be a friend to yourself and others will soon become
A friend to you
1127
Love yourself and treat yourself well
Everything else will fall in place
He who is his own friend is a friend to all
1128
Some people who enter our lives
Change it forever
Be choosy about who you
Let into your life
1129
It is better to be wounded than to walk around in armor
You may be protected but you will feel nothing
The only way to never be disappointed
Is to never expect anything

1130
Vulnerability is often the price of growth
If you put up a wall or live in a shell
You may avoid pain but won't experience joy
Growth is only possible with pain
1131
Enduring others pain if you love them
Is more difficult than enduring our own
1132
Friends are the siblings we should have had
Friends are siblings we give ourselves
Associate with people you choose to call brother
Associate with people you choose to call sister
1133
Home is where your heart is
Home is where you want to be
Home is where if you go there
They have to take you in
1144
Children need much love and attention, give it to them
But remember regardless of our age
We all need about the same amount or love and attention
Be careful not to starve the adults in your life, or yourself
1145
People judge you by the friends you keep
And by the enemies you make
Be careful about the company you keep
And wary of the enemies you make
1146
It does not matter so much where you live
As how you live there and who you live with
1147
You are rich according to what you are
Not according to what you have
You are rich according to your friends and family
1148
A kind word need not cost much
The price of praise can be cheap
With half a loaf and an empty cup
You can be and have a good friend

1149
Listening to someone
Is sometimes all the help they need
A gentle ear can be a great gift
Be kind enough to listen
1150
Seek first to understand, then to be understood
However it requires a certain ability level
For a person to understand anything you or themselves
Some people are too stupid to understand anything
1151
Make yourself worth knowing
Make yourself someone
Who you would like to know
If you were someone else, would you be your friend
1152
The greatest duty we have in life
The greatest gift we give our children
The duty we most often neglect
Is the duty to be happy
1153
The best life is led by those who choose to be happy
In being jolly you are doing right
This will increase your circle of kinsmen
To be unjolly is a crime, against your children
1154
Life is too short and love is too precious
To waste it on imaginary beings
Love your family, love your friends
Let fantasy beings fend for themselves
1155
A man guarded himself from everyone family and friends
No one ever tricked him he was a lonely miserable man
He who does not trust, will not be trusted
It is better to be deceived by a friend, than to mistrust one
1156
It hurts to find trust and faith
Placed in a false friend was waste
The fault was theirs, not yours
It is better to be deceived by a friend, than to mistrust one

1157
If you know a friend you can fully trust
Go often to his home
Grass and brambles grow quickly
Upon the untrodden track
1158
You are here a short time
Immortality is your children
Immortality is their children
A strong family lives forever
1159
Man was not made to be alone
When several come together
The holy force grows
And the ancestors are glad
1160
Cherish those near you
Never be first to break with a friend
Care eats at him who no longer can
Open his heart to another
1161
Good parents love their children and hold their babies tight
As soon as they are born you must begin to let them go
A loving mother makes for loving children
The true test of a family is time
1162
Do things with your children
While they still want to do things with you
1163
Don't let your children do things
That would cause you to dislike them
The most foolish and saddest thing in the world
Is for parents to raise bad children
1164
Nothing is so strong as gentleness
Nothing is so gentle as real strength

1165
The love your parents gave to you
It can never be returned
It was meant to be passed down
Pass it to your children, and they will pass it to theirs
1166
All parents want good for their children
Strong, smart and kind of heart
Part of a parent's job is to
Get out of the way of their children
1167
A child is a blessing though born late in life
To a father no longer alive
Stones would seldom stand by the road
If children did not set them there
1168
The meaning of life is found
In one's children
Your friends and children should be treated well
It is a shame to do otherwise
1169
They said the boy had problems sitting still and quiet
The wise old man said to his parents
There is nothing wrong with that boy
That one hundred acres would not cure
1170
The good king Beowulf said, life is better shared
Ring giver, glory winner, treasure taker, it was no matter
It's not what you have, but who you have
And more importantly who has you
1171
It is not what you have
But who you have
And who has you
This is what makes you rich

1172
It is important to have friends and family
Good people of like mind you can trust
People you can show yourself to
Bitter becomes a man among his enemies
For he must always hide his heart
1173
Instead of loving your enemies
Treat your friends a little better
The time spent loving a tyrant
Could be used loving your family
1174
Anyone who says raising children
Is not the most difficult job in the world
Is not doing it right
1175
Always leave home
With a tender good-bye and loving words
1176
Treat your children the way
You wanted your parents to treat you
Do not do to them that which would cause you pain
If the same was done to you
1177
Kids need more hugs then they need things
You should always have more love than money
Your children need your presence
More than they need your presents
1178
Time spent with your children is not wasted
1179
Make peace with imperfection
The world is filled with it
And you will find much of it
You may even be a part of it
1180
A work of art can be perfect
But filled with imperfections

1181
The sound of laughing children is a blessing
A place with the sound of laughing children
Is a blessed place
The sound of laughing children is sometimes all it takes
To make a home
1182
Children follow examples not advice
Children learn by imitation not words
Your children copy everything you do
Every deed you do, your children do
1183
In a friendship because you share
The good times are double
The bad times are cut in half
And that is a pretty good deal
1184
The greatest good you can do for another
Is not to do them a good service
Is not to show them how good you are
It is to reveal to someone their own goodness
1185
A true friend never gets in your way
Unless you are falling down
1186
The most important thing parents can teach their children
Is how to get along, without them
1187
Good times are better when shared
It doubles the joy
And can cut the sorry in half
1188
Friendship is like a garden
It needs constant care to be maintained
1189
A child is like a garden
That needs constant care and attention
It needs more than just planting
In order to grow correctly

1190
Teach your children to eat right and be healthy
Teach them how to select a proper mate
Teach them how to life without you
Teach them how to surpass you
1191
Encourage your children to surpass you
The greatest gift a child can give a parent
Is to surpass them
And this is the greatest hope a parent has for a child
1192
Great friendships last until the grave
And the greatest last beyond
1193
Don't conceal love
In all of the world
It is one of the most beautiful things
To hide it is a shame
1194
Some things need to be said
Do not let important things be unsaid
Say what is important
Take the time needed to express love
1195
When you really like someone, tell them
Otherwise it is a waste, it might as well not be
To get the full value of joy
You must have somebody to share it with
1196
Make sure your children are children
When they are young
They are not young, very long
And they are not children, very long
1197
Teach your children
To live their own lives
And the best way to do this
Is to set the example by living your life

1198
Treasure your children for what they are
Not for what you want them to be
Do not curse them for what they are not
Treasure your children for who they are
1199
If you have one true friend in all the world
You have more than your fair share
1200
You cannot betray a friend
Without betraying yourself
He who betrays friendship for personal gain
Burns a beautiful picture to get the ashes
1201
Since we expect more from friends
It takes us longer to forgive them
Friends are so valuable that sometimes
We might want to consider that option
1202
Before blame, see if you can excuse
1203
Say positive things to the people you love everyday
Say important things,
Don't waste your words or time with loved ones
On unimportant things
1204
As the tree falls and rots, having neither needles nor bark
So is the fate of a friendless man
So is the fate of a man without family
Why should he live long
1205
Bare is the back of he with no brothers
1206
Hold your child's hand every chance you get
They grow up so fast they aren't babies very long
Very soon they will no longer want to hold your hand

1207
You cannot undo anything that you did in the past
But you can learn from it
Even the gods can't change the past
Do you think you can do more than a god
1208
Hating someone is like drinking poison
And expecting the other person to die
If you cannot effectively hurt your opponent
At least don't poison yourself
1209
The energy we use to get even
Might be used in getting ahead
Living well is the best revenge
The best revenge is living well
1210
Regret of the things we did can be tempered with time
But the pain of what we did not do
The pain of what we are not
That is inconsolable
1211
Memories are your most valuable possessions
You should spend a lifetime building that treasure
Spend your time, making good memories
So you will have joy in your old age
1212
You are old longer than you are young
Plan your life accordingly
No one seems to tell the young this fact
Though all old people know its true
1213
Invest in your health
It is probably the best investment you can make
1214
Take care of your body
It is the only home you have
Think long and hard about this
It should last you a lifetime

1215
Live in health and think clearly
Then look back at all with joy
1216
How old would you be if you did not know your age
Sometimes this knowledge can stand in your way
Perhaps your sweetest songs are still unsung
1217
You only feel old
If you have nothing to do
If you have nothing to dream
If you have nothing to look forward to
1218
There comes a time in every man's life
When the only person he fools is himself
1219
Time is more precious than things
Time is the most precious thing you have
1220
How you spend your time
Is how you live your life
When your time is wasted, your life is wasted
Controlling your life means controlling, your time
1221
Time should be spent solving problems
Not worrying about them
1222
An hour wasted, a minute wasted, a second wasted
Can never be regained and is lost forever
Every situation and every moment
Is of infinite value
1223
Each moment is too precious to waste
There is no greater crime, than waste of time
There is no greater loss, than loss of time
Time is not for sale

1224
If you kill time, it will eventually kill you
Do not kill your life
Since you cannot make more time
Spend the time that you have wisely
1225
Lost time is never found again
Time is the fairest and harshest of masters
Time is the most perishable and precious
The most valuable of all your assets
1226
Life is not a problem to be solved
It is a gift to be enjoyed
Life is not a destination
It is a journey to enjoy along the way
1227
Laughing makes you live longer
1228
Home is where the heart is
It does you good to know where your home is
It does you good to know where your heart is
1229
Take the time needed to express love
The time to express love is now
1230
Say positive things to the people you love, everyday
Say important things daily
Don't waste your words or time with loved ones
Saying unimportant things
1231
You can only perceive real beauty
In a person as they grow older
We get not better or worse as we age
Only more like ourselves
1232
It is a paradox that the surest sign of old age
Is loneliness, but a major cause of old age is loneliness
The surest sign of age is loneliness
And it's chief cause

1233
Life is a gift but really a loan
Use it while you have it
Use it knowing one day you must return it
Life is not the kind of gift you get to keep
1234
The wise have listened to my counsel
You will fare well if you follow it,
It will help you much if you heed it
It is for you if you need it
1235
So were your ancestors established
Sons and daughters of sky and earth
With fire in our eyes and glory on our foreheads
Living flames, a nation of heroes, we walked with the gods
1236
Better not to offer than to over pledge
As a gift always demands a gift
Better not to slay than to slay too many
Thus did Odin speak before the world began
1237
Now I will answer what you ask of the runes
Graven by gods, made for our folk
Sent by the powerful sage
It is best for men to be silent and listen
1238
Nine worlds of power, twenty four songs
And more, I learned from that famous well
Poured me a draught of precious mead
Mixed with inspiration, knowledge and wisdom
1239
Wounded I hung on a wind-swept gallows
For nine long nights
Pierced by a spear pledged to Odin
Myself offered to myself
1240
The wisest know not from whence spring
The roots of that ancient tree
Fed by the waters of the well
Holding nine worlds

1241
They gave me no bread they gave me no meat
No water, no mead, nor aid did I have
Down to the deepest depths I peered
Until I spied the runes
1242
I looked down and with a loud cry
On my last breath, I took up the runes
Then dizzy and fainting
From that tree, I fell
1243
Well-being I won and wisdom too
From a word to a word I was lead to a word
From a deed to a deed I was lead to a deed
This is how I grew in strength and wisdom
1244
Runes you will find and readable staves
Symbols and signs of might and power
Very strong staves, very stout staves
Useful if you are wise enough
1245
Blood stained staves made by mighty powers
Graven by the prophetic ones
Fashioned by the high ones
For the use of our people
1246
For the gods, for the elves, for the dwarves
For the giants, and for the wisest of men
Some I found, some were gifts and some I carved myself
Arranged for our people and given to you
1247
Powers from before man shaped them
It is time to sing from the seat of the wise
Of what at Urd's well I saw in silence
I thought on long, worked and learned
1248
Runes heard spoken, counsels revealed in the hall
I listened carefully and heard this

1249
Know how to cut them, know how to read them
Know how to stain them, know how to prove them
Know how to evoke them, know how to score them
Know how to send them, know how to offer them
Know how to ask them, know how to understand them
1250
The first rune I know is Fehu, wealth, counting
Cattle, gold, silver money or material possessions
Riches can be burdensome and cause strife
A wolf lives in the woods, he who hoards has little
Remember whatever you own, owns you
1251
I know a second called Uruz, the Auroch
That sons of men must learn who wish to be healers
It is primeval power, wild and strong life force
The strength of the Auroch, the storm, the primal in us all
1252
I know a third called Thurisaz the thorn
If my need be great and danger near
It will warn me of spears or enemy swords
Their weapons will make no wounds
I can send to destroy my enemies
1253
I know a fourth Ansuz, poetry, hidden knowledge
It will free me if foes bind me, bonds will burst from me
It is wisdom, truth and deeper meaning, understanding
Bonds burst from my mind, bonds burst from my body
Wisdom and knowledge free me understanding frees me
1254
I know a fifth Raido travel action
Movement do I master
No flying arrow, aimed to bring harm can reach me
Adventure journey where I need to be
Movement where I need to go

1255
I know a sixth Kenaz, opening
Receiving, reveling changing
It will save me if I need transformation
Change and rebirth, new beginnings
It turns the spell, the hater is harmed, not me
1256
I know a seventh Gebo, exchange, the sharing one
Exchange, gifts partnership, friendship
It will bond our friendship strong
This will make for mutual friendship
As long as both shall live
1257
I know an eighth Wunjo that all are glad of
Glory, joy, prize, happiness, comfort, celebration
If hate, envy or strife, fester in the heart of a warrior
It will soon calm and cure him
Joy and victory can be won
A waving flag of victory for all
1258
I know a ninth Hagalz, Hail
Storm, harsh, the coldest grain
It can destroy and lay waste to crops
It can destroy an enemy too, but be careful
The plow is a destructive force but needed
Before the field grows again
1259
I know a tenth Nauthiz, need
If troublesome deficiency, wants or lack
Afflict you or yours, house, cattle or stead
I can work it so the need is removed
1260
I know an eleventh Isa, Ice
Cold freezing standing still frozen passage
Ice that blocks the way must be dealt with
Before anything can be done
Ice can freeze, bind, solidify, stop or harden
Use it with care, spells made strong

1261
I know a twelfth Jera all year
Planting and harvest cycle complete
Summer and winter both halves
Complete wheel of the year, beginning and end
The most perfect cycle in its shape
1262
I know a thirteenth Eiwaz
Universe, the axis of the world tree
Through all the worlds the bridge
The backbone of the worlds the backbone of a man
It touches all much more than fools see
1263
I know a fourteenth Perthro, luck
Unknowing, fate, chance, hidden meaning
The high ones, elves and gods, can master their fate
Strong men can shape it, little can the nitwit control
Even the gods must deal with chance
1264
I know a fifteenth Elhaz, Elk horn
The sacred place geese go, the sanctuary were elk hide
Hallowing, protection, it is a safe place I go
Touching gods power, prowess to elves
A sacred symbol a sacred stance
The gesture is itself a prayer
1265
I know a sixteenth Sowelu, The Sun
Waves, life, the Sun's rays, radiation of energy
If I see a girl I can turn her thoughts
Melt her heart and touch her mind
The movement and force between all things
1266
I know a seventeenth Teiwaz, Spear
Straight justice, proper action right and unyielding
Victory, no matter the cost, right action no matter the price
Raw courage, doing the right thing
More than most are capable of

1267
I know an eighteenth Berkana, Pregnant
Spring, birth and blossoming hope
Motherhood a gift I hide from all
Except the love, who lies in my arms
Life conceived, started well, birth of new beginnings

1268
I know a nineteenth Ehwaz the horse twins
If you need to do more than you can alone
Cooperate with something larger than yourself
And you may accomplish great things
If you can work with another and align yourself
Then become more careful not to lose yourself

1269
I know a twentieth Mannaz, mankind
The collective folk, all the tribe
God's power in you and people
It is potential for us to be
A raised banner for us all

1270
I know twenty-first Laguz, water
It takes many forms, all shapes it can become
It touches all things and makes up all life
Water is everywhere and needed daily
The universal solvent and it can be deep
Deeper than the half-wit realize

1271
I know a twenty-second Inguz, DNA
Pollination and fertilization
The successful coming together of new life
The wrapping of life is a delicate thing
And care is still needed to bring successful birth

1272
I know a twenty-third Dagaz, Day and night
A 24-hour cycle, today right now
A point in time, a moment, one turn of the earth
It can be an instant or a moment or a day
It will help me if timing is needed
It can aid me now it can aid me today

1273
I know a twenty-forth Othila, roots
If I am lost I can find my homeland
If I forget who I am I can remember
My ancestors walk with me
My ancestors talk with me
My roots to them go back so far
It gives me strength and stability to know my heritage
1274
So is answered what you ask of the runes
To learn to sing them will take a long time
Helpful they are if you understand them
Useful if you use them, needful if you need them
1275
The High one has spoken for the good of man
Words of wisdom and strength for our people
Needful for men to know, unneedful for trolls to know
Sayings of the High One, uttered in the hall
1276
Weave your destiny and claim what is yours
You are not the creation of circumstances
Circumstances are the creation of you
You can be more powerful than matter
You must go past the point where luck can befall you
1277
Hail to the speaker, hail to the knower
Joy to those who have listened
Delight to he, who has understood
Blessings to those changed by what they have learned